# BREAKING THE SILENCE

# BREAKING THE SILENCE

## A Guide to Help Children with Complicated Grief—
## Suicide, Homicide, AIDS, Violence, and Abuse

## LINDA GOLDMAN

ACCELERATED DEVELOPMENT
*A member of the Taylor & Francis Group*

| USA | Production Office: | ACCELERATED DEVELOPMENT |
| | | *A member of the Taylor & Francis Group* |
| | | 1101 Vermont Avenue, NW, Suite 200 |
| | | Washington, DC 20005 |
| | | Tel.: 202-289-2174 |
| | | Fax: 202-289-3665 |
| | Distribution Center: | ACCELERATED DEVELOPMENT |
| | | *A member of the Taylor & Francis Group* |
| | | 1900 Frost Road, Suite 101 |
| | | Bristol, PA 19007 |
| | | Tel.: 215-785-5800 |
| | | Fax: 215-785-5515 |
| UK | | Taylor & Francis, Ltd. |
| | | 1 Gunpowder Square |
| | | London EC4A 3DE |
| | | Tel.: 0171 583 0490 |
| | | Fax: 0171 583 0581 |

**BREAKING THE SILENCE: A Guide to Help Children with Complicated Grief—Suicide, Homicide, AIDS, Violence, and Abuse**

2 3 4 5 6 7 8 9 0 BRBR 9 8 7

This book was designed and set in Times Roman by Gaston Originals. Technical development and editing by Cindy Long. Cover design by Arthur Goldberg. Printing and binding by Braun-Brumfield, Inc.

A CIP catalog record for this book is available from the British Library.
∞ The paper in this publication meets the requirements of the ANSI Standard Z39.48-1984 (Permanence of Paper)

**Library of Congress Cataloging-in-Publication Data**
Goldman, Linda.
   Breaking the silence: a guide to help children with complicated grief, suicide, homicide, aids, violence, and abuse/ Linda Goldman.
      p. cm.
   Includes bibliographical references and index.
   1. Grief in children. 2. Bereavement in children. 3. Grief therapy. 4. Abused children—Psychology. 5. Victims of crimes—Psychology. I. Title.
BF723.G75G64 1996
155.9 '37'083—dc20

96-13029

CIP

ISBN 1-56032-434-1

# DEDICATION

To Katy, Andrew, Chet, and Luke

I have grown to know and love you all through the loving eyes of your parents.  I have grown to respect and admire your life's courage, as children and as human beings on this planet.

I have come to see that *who* you are is very separate from *how* and *why* you died.  Thank you for teaching me this lesson.

Linda

Anecdotes that appear throughout this guide contain names and stories that have been modified to maintain privacy. The children, adults, animals, and scenery in the photographs may not relate specifically to the material on the pages where they appear.

# TABLE OF CONTENTS

## PART I
### COMPLICATED GRIEF

## PART II
### BREAKING THE SILENCE

## PART III

### TECHNIQUES

# PREFACE

There are no throwaway people. Every person on the planet is recyclable. Every person is worthy of help. Sometimes we think *those* people are not good enough, *those* people don't count as much, *those* people have so many problems that no amount of energy we give them can help them find another way of experiencing life. *Those* people are us. Our interconnectedness grows daily to the point that a murder, a suicide, an AIDS victim, an airplane crash, a terrorist's bombing, cannot help but spill over into our lives. So opening the door for others opens the doors for ourselves.

I'm reminded of a story I heard that touched my heart. I hope it will touch yours. . . .

One night a man was walking on the beach. He saw thousands of starfish washed to the shore. A little boy was picking them up one at a time and throwing them back into the ocean. The man walked up to him and asked him, "What are you doing?" "Why are you doing this?" and "What does it matter?" As the little boy picked up the next starfish, held it up to the moonlight, and got ready to throw it back into the ocean, he replied, "It matters to this one."

# INTRODUCTION

Linda Goldman has boldly broken the silence. Children in America today (as well as in Ireland, Bosnia, Rwanda, etc.) are bombarded by violence. It is on the news, in the video arcades, and in the streets. That is not news. Children are suffering both immediate and long-term effects of that violence. That is not news either. They *all* need help and *can be* helped. This is the news Linda Goldman delivers in this book. This is a book for professionals, parents, and other caring adults who touch the lives of children caught up in the trauma of their existence.

Many of us, uncomfortable as we may be with the day-to-day psychological traumas of our young people, find it difficult to address complicated grief—grief that results from senseless violence, abuse, social stigma, homicide, and suicide. Exposed to a brief but overwhelming experience, a child will retreat behind an invisible wall erected to protect what remains of the psyche. Left to their own devices for a period of time, such traumatized children learn to function with little interference from the original disturbance. However, it is at a great psychological cost. Personality patterns that may be dysfunctional in some contexts become established and maintained because of the security these patterns provide in avoiding the experience of trauma and its sequelae.

Alternatively, chronic psychic fatigue is more likely to develop in children who live in the war zones that many urban environments and suburban televisions have become; in children whose personal tragedies of parental suicide or homicide occur in a life impoverished by lack of financial and/or social support; or in children who are abused over a number of years. Chronic pyschic fatigue is an absence of hope; a bleak future, if any; an expectation of early death; apathy; low aspirations; impulsivity; and an emphasis on immediate gratification often resulting in substance abuse. We see these children in the schools, the day-care centers, doctors' offices, and as clients in various social service programs (e.g., AFDC, protective services, and juvenile services).

We see them, but we may ignore them or their grief. In some instances, we ignore them because they do not appear to be doing too badly considering what has happened in their young lives. In other instances, we ignore them because we do not know what to do for them—we do not know how to break the silence, to get beyond the wall and provide comfort and healing so that the children can move forward.

Linda Goldman has written this book for all people who work with children experiencing complicated grief. She helps us see that we should not assume that time will heal the child. She provides us with concrete guidelines by which to identify the problems of children suffering from complicated grief. Most of all, she provides a conceptually based and structured procedure, descriptions of a wealth of concrete therapeutic techniques, and sources for additional ones. For those who deal with children, especially those who deal with children chronically exposed to violence, and wish to help these children, this book is an invaluable resource.

*Alfred Lucco, Ph.D.*
Child and Family Therapist
Associate Professor, School of Social Work
University of Maryland at Baltimore (UMAB)

# ACKNOWLEDGMENTS

I would like to thank

my husband, Michael, for his love and continuing support for my work;

my son, Jon, for his boundless ideas and encouragement;

Ellen Zinner, PsyD., for her invaluable work in editing;

Beverly Celotta, Ph.D., Lori Wiener, Ph.D., Joan Leibermann, M.D., and Laura MacKenzie, for their expertise;

Al Lucco, Ph.D., for the knowledge he has shared with me and his continuing guidance;

all of the children and adults who bravely shared their experiences, materials, and photographs in order to help other children.

# PART I
# COMPLICATED GRIEF

# Chapter 1

## WHAT IS CHILDREN'S COMPLICATED GRIEF?

■ Terrorists blow up buildings and murder kids and adults
■ Mom kills Dad ■ Dad kills Mom ■ Brother is stabbed outside home
■ Friend hangs himself ■ Uncle is murdered in drive-by shooting
■ Sister gets AIDS ■ Drunk driver kills teacher ■ Grandmother dies of
sudden heart attack ■ Child is kidnapped from home and murdered
■ Grandfather shoots himself in head ■ Teacher is arrested for rape
■ Mom drowns two children ■ Baby-sitter beats infant to death

## A LOOK AT GRIEF

My first book, *Life and Loss: A Guide to Help Grieving Children*, concentrates on normal grief work with children. The four tasks of normal grief—understanding, grieving, commemorating, and moving on—are presented and explained. The emphasis of *Life and Loss* is on recognizing and understanding the denial that so often accompanies loss and grief.

Death is viewed culturally as the enemy of life. Even though we know it cannot be avoided, we generally push it out of our minds and live in denial of its everyday presence. Consequently, we feel unprepared to deal with death and become shocked and traumatized when we are forced to face it. Sooner or later, each adult and child will be called upon to face the loss of a loved one. Our culture does not always provide the support and openness needed to accept *normal* grief, and the complications involved with issues of suicide, homicide, AIDS, abuse, and violence cry out for a "new way of seeing" in our society. If we, as a society, can see differently, so can our children.

The focus of *Breaking the Silence* is to provide a guide for caring adults to help children with these complicated issues. The scarcity of children's works on the topics of suicide, homicide, AIDS, violence, and abuse only magnifies the need to create a resource that gives adults and children *the words to use to break this prison of silence and denial that is so much a part of today's culture.* This prison of silence and denial was not created by the children. They were born into it. A 12-year-old client who refuses to tell her friend that her father died for fear she will have to tell her friend *how* her father died faces a prison of silence locked shut by society. An 8-year-old who continually runs away from school, shouting and screaming to teachers and administrators his desire to not live any longer, is told by the health care system that there is no hurry for him to be seen because he is just being manipulative. Couldn't suicide be the ultimate manipulation? And who would ultimately be responsible? We (society) would be. Let's get these kids help.

 We need to open a door and allow the children to breathe freely the fresh air of truth. By bringing these subjects into the light of day without fear and shame, we can create a healing environment for communicating loss and grief.

Hopefully, *Breaking the Silence* will help accomplish this purpose. First, adults will be given specific ideas, techniques, resources, and materials to work with children in each area of complicated grief. Second, adults will be given the specific words to use with children and ways to initiate discussions of these anxiety-producing topics. Third, caring adults will be given the information and tools to help them separate the child from the circumstances surrounding his or her loss and grief. These complications of grief must be recognized and dealt with before the normal grief can be acknowledged and released.

Despite the complicated circumstances of suicide, homicide, AIDS, violence, and abuse, the underlying process of grief is universal and timeless. As horrendous as these circumstances are, they could happen to any one of us at any time.

 Photographs of nature, animals, and children are interwoven throughout this book to remind us continually that the cycle of life and death is ever present and ongoing. The death of someone or something we love is a normal and natural process of life that we all will experience.

Hopefully the photos included will provide an ongoing reminder that these "unnatural events" exist in daily life and need to be addressed and dealt with openly. The "unnatural" has become a very "normal" part of the world of today's children. By recognizing this, caring adults can break through the silent shame and stigma of complicated grief with children and help them reach the underlying feelings of normal loss and grief that everyone shares.

## WHAT IS NORMAL GRIEF?

*Grief* is defined as a normal, internalized reaction to the loss of a person, thing, or idea. It is our emotional response to loss.

*Bereavement* is the state of having lost something, whether it be significant other, significant things, or our own sense of will.

*Mourning* means taking the internal experience of grief and expressing it outside ourselves. It is the cultural expression of grief, as seen in traditional or creative rituals. Traditional rituals refer to ones that are sanctioned culturally, such as funerals. Creative rituals can be writing a letter to the deceased and then destroying it. Rituals are the behaviors we use to do grief work.

Goldman,1994, p. 21

These definitions are explained further in my first book, *Life and Loss: A Guide to Help Grieving Children*. A brief overview of normal grief is important in order to differentiate between normal grief and the many complications that can occur. Sandra Fox, in her book *Good Grief* (1988), defined the four psychological tasks of grief as follows:

 Understanding
Grieving
Commemorating
Moving On

The first task is **understanding**. Kids need to make sense of loss at whatever developmental stage they experience it. Children have different developmental perceptions of death. Young children feel death is reversible, and many times their magical thinking creates feelings of guilt that they may have caused a death. A cliche such as "your Mom is better off dead; she was suffering so much" can only inhibit the grief process of a child who misses his or her mom.

The second task is **grieving.** Children will experience physical, emotional, cognitive, and behavioral symptoms in normal grief. These normal grief signals cover a range from stomachaches and nightmares to poor grades and hostility toward friends.

 ## NORMAL GRIEF SYMPTOMS

Child continually *retells events* about loved one and his or her death.

Child *feels loved one is present* in some way and *speaks of him or her in the present tense.*

Child *dreams about loved one* and *longs* to be with him or her.

Child *experiences nightmares and sleeplessness.*

Child *cannot concentrate* on schoolwork.

Child *appears at times not to feel anything.*

Child *is preoccupied with death* and *worries excessively about health issues.*

Child *is afraid to be left alone.*

Child *cries often* at unexpected times.

Child *bed-wets* or *loses appetite.*

Child *idealizes loved one* and *assumes mannerisms.*

Child *becomes "class bully"* or *"class clown."*

Child *feels headaches and stomachaches.*

Child *rejects old friends, withdraws, or acts out.*

The third task is **commemorating**. Children need to find concrete ways to make death and other losses meaningful. By lighting a candle, writing a poem, planting a flower, or sending a balloon into the air, grieving children can express their grief symbolically.

The fourth task is **moving on**. Moving on means that the child will not forget a brother who was murdered but will find an inner place for the love for the brother that lives inside and is carried throughout life. When a child is ready to revisit the playground where he and his brother played, he has moved to another level of grief work.

Grief is as unique as each individual child. Yet it is important to understand normal grief principles in order to recognize grief even when a child may be unable to express feelings. The intensity, frequency, and duration of normal grief symptoms are good indicators of *underlying complications* leading to prolonged or unresolved grief. These complications may stem from competing or conflicting issues that inhibit the expression of normal grief. The child's grief process becomes frozen in time.

## WHAT IS COMPLICATED GRIEF?

 When life issues are unexpressed or unacknowledged, they become locked in frozen blocks of time.

Frozen blocks of time stop normal grief and deny a child the ability to grieve. This can feel to a child as if life stops and time stands still. The natural flow of feelings is inhibited. There is no movement forward until the issues are resolved and the feelings are released. Suicide, homicide, AIDS, abuse, and violence are familiar examples of situations that lead to complicated grief.

The grief process is normal and natural after a loss. When children become stuck in a frozen block of time, they are denied access to this normal and natural flowing process. Overwhelmed by frozen feelings, the grief process seems to be on hold or nonexistent. The child is not in touch with his or her feelings of grief, or those feelings are ambivalent and in conflict.

In complicated grief, it is as if an unexpressed or unresolved important life issue—a frozen block of time—has created a wall of ice between the child and his or her grief. Our job is to help melt that wall.

## CATEGORIES THAT CONTRIBUTE TO COMPLICATED GRIEF

### Sudden or Traumatic Death

Sudden or traumatic death can include murder, suicide, a fatal accident, or sudden fatal illness. Immediately an *unstable environment* is created in the child's home. Children feel *confusion* over these kinds of death. Desire for *revenge* often is experienced after a murder or fatal accident. *Rage* and/or *guilt* emerge against the person who has committed suicide. *Terror* of violence and death unfolds, and the child feels *shock and disbelief* that suddenly this death has occurred.

### Social Stigma of Death

*Social stigma and shame* frequently accompany deaths related to AIDS, suicide, and homicide. Children as well as adults often feel too *embarrassed* to speak of these issues. They remain *silent* out of *fear of being ridiculed or ostracized*. These suppressed feelings get projected outwardly onto others in the form of *rage* or inwardly projected toward themselves in the form of *self-hatred*. Often these kids feel *lonely and isolated*. They cannot grieve normally because they have *not separated* the loss of the deceased from the way the deceased died.

### Multiple Losses

Multiple losses can produce a deep *fear of abandonment and self-doubt* in children. The death of a single parent is a good example of a multiple loss. When the only remaining parent of a child dies, the death can cause this child to be forced to move from the home, the rest of his or her family and friends, the school, and the community. The child is *shocked* at this *sudden and complete change of lifestyle and surroundings*, and may *withdraw* or *become terrified of future abandonment*. *Nightmares* and/or *bed-wetting* could appear.

### Past Relationship to the Deceased

When a child has been *abused, neglected, or abandoned* by a loved one, there often are *ambivalent feelings* when the loved one's death occurs. A 5-year-old girl whose alcoholic father sexually abused her felt great *conflict* when that parent died. Part of her may have felt *relieved*, even glad, to be rid of the abuse yet *ashamed* to say those feelings out loud. She may carry the *secret* of the abuse and become locked into that memory and be unable to grieve. Children often feel *guilt, fear, abandonment, or depression* if grief of a loved one is complicated by an unresolved past relationship.

**Grief Process of the Surviving Parent or Caretaker**

If the surviving parent is unable to mourn, there is *no role model* for the child. A *closed environment* stops the grief process. Many times the surviving parent finds it *too difficult* to watch his or her child grieve. The parent may be unable to grieve himself or herself or unwilling to recognize the child's pain. Feelings become denied and expression of these feelings withheld. The surviving parent may well become an *absentee parent* because of his or her own overwhelming grief, producing feelings of *abandonment and isolation* in the child. Children often *fear* something will happen to this parent or to themselves and, as a result, become *overprotective* of the parent and other loved ones.

How can we protect the children from the barrage of complicated grief that fills today's world and lies waiting for them inside their homes and outside their doorsteps? The children of the 90s face a grief far more horrifying than we did as children. Alder (1994) reported that today's children face the loss of the protection of the adult world. Grief always has and always will exist as a part of life. People are born, they live, they die—an ongoing part of the life cycle. Too many of today's kids face real circumstances that do not permit them to grieve normally. They are disrupted from this process by such issues as murder, suicide, abuse, violence, and AIDS.

All situations or circumstances that breed fear, shame, and terror cut off the grief process and result in children caught unexpectedly in "frozen blocks of time."

## FROZEN BLOCKS OF TIME

"Frozen blocks of time" is an important concept underlying complicated grief. Children experiencing complicated grief usually feel unable to break free from overwhelming feelings experienced at the time of their trauma. They become imprisoned in these feelings if they are not given the freedom to work through their grief.

We, as caring adults, need to facilitate a "meltdown process" whereby children can be comfortable enough to reexperience all the overwhelming feelings they felt at the time of their loss.

1. We can do this by *seeing the child in the present* and seeing his or her behaviors as a cry for help. This frozen state of denial and endless searching for what was not available at the time of the loss must be replaced by trust in a process of remembering so that his or her pain is not carried into adulthood.

2. Then we can *create a safe environment* for the child as a friend, an advocate, or a guide to walk the child through his or her grief work when ready.

3. Next, we *become a helper in remembering* when it feels safe for the child to remember the overwhelming feelings felt at the time of the loss.

4. Lastly, we need to *provide a space to reexperience the denied feelings.* Each time children can release the fears, the tears, the terror, the rage, the guilt, the self-hatred, and the love they felt at the time of their loss, they are taking a step on the path toward their own healing. *This is the essence of complicated grief work and the thread that binds everything we will discuss in this book.*

## MELTDOWN PROCESS

Too often children are told or given the following message: "Don't talk about it! Don't think about it! Don't feel about it! It makes me feel uncomfortable, and you as a child have a job to do—keep the adults in your life comfortable. We don't want to remember our own feelings or our own pain."

Often children are taught to put a bell jar over their feelings and live in separate worlds of isolation to please the adult world. If children continue to avoid their own pain, they again and again will find themselves re-creating situations that attempt to access these hidden feelings. The following are three examples:

1. Sandy was a young girl who came to see me with her aunt and uncle. They were concerned that she had not grieved the death of her mother. She was withdrawn. She could not look at me and did not speak. Her guardians said she had not cried over her mother's death. Sandy was 6 years old when her mom died of a sudden heart attack, and Sandy was taken away from her home, her friends, her family, her school, and her community and brought to live in a new environment with which she was not familiar. As a result of these multiple losses, she was reluctant to speak. It took several months to establish the trust to begin the meltdown process.

2. Another example was Rachel, a 29-year-old woman who began grief therapy because she had been overwhelmed by feelings of loss since childhood, appeared learning disabled, and had suffered from depression and relied

on antidepressants for many years. After exploring her childhood, it became clear that her mother's illness and death when Rachel was 11 was very much unresolved. Her feelings had not been heard or acknowledged. Her father remarried quickly and moved to another state with Rachel losing friends, school, and safety as well as her mom all within 1 year. The painful feelings of loss as a child remained unresolved and plagued her in adulthood.

3. A third example demonstrating this meltdown process was in the case of Bonnie, a woman who came for grief therapy in her 60s. Her husband had died, and eventually she began to date a man. She came into my office one day terrified that this man was going to kill her cat. As we explored the facts, we saw the man had never shown evidence of violence toward her or her cat. Again, we went back to her childhood and realized that she was terrorized at age 5 by a raging stepfather. She learned and feared that anger might be powerful enough to kill her, or her anger could be powerful enough to kill someone else. She began to see how her childhood trauma had been carried far into adulthood in an unconscious way. With this realization, she had begun the meltdown process.

These examples were chosen because they illustrate that individuals ranging from 9 to 65 can be frozen in time in their childhoods. How much better might life have been had the complicated grief issues been resolved while these people were still children? Each one of these people held stored up fear and pain. This stored fear and pain can be projected inward and result in self-hatred or even suicide. This stored fear and pain also can be projected outward onto others, resulting in violence, abuse, or homicide.

The meltdown process allows individuals who have become frozen in time by a deep trauma *to reexperience their feelings* in a way that they were not able to do at the time of their loss. For Sandy, a *safe environment* allowed her to feel secure enough to remember and reexperience the overwhelming emotions of sadness she felt at age 6 over her mom's fatal heart attack. The process afforded Rachel *a space to remember* her mom's unbearable illness and death due to cancer when Rachel was 11. For Bonnie, it offered *permission to feel* the terror of a 5-year-old confronted by a raging alcoholic parent. No longer did these people feel the need to pretend about or deny these childhood events. By bringing their own personal horrors into the light of day, the fear from being trapped in time was lifted.

## FACILITATING MELTDOWN

We, as caring adults, need to achieve an openness about these previously closed topics by

1. stressing the underlying belief that we always need to *separate* the person who died from the way that person died to truly grieve the person's death; and
2. *defining* suicide, homicide, AIDS, violence, and abuse to children in simple and direct language that eliminates judgment.

By separating and defining, we can help the adult world hold those thought forms and re-create adults' own concepts of the unspeakable by using the language of children. For example, children need to make sense of death and, even more, of suicide. If we define death for children as "when the body stops working," then we can define suicide for children as "when someone chooses to make his or her body not work anymore."

So often I have found in private practice as a grief therapist that the *adult caregiver's fear and shame is the major factor in noncommunication with children*. A mom's terror of not having the words to tell her 9-year-old that his older brother died of a drug overdose locks herself and her family into a hidden secret and their inability to express it. When a mom and I can successfully role-play a dialogue with her 7-year-old son telling him of his father's suicide, we have eliminated a great deal of the perceived terror that we adults feel. We are then better able to communicate to children.

Our inability to discuss these topics openly with kids creates an atmosphere of secrecy, loneliness, and isolation far more damaging than the actual death of someone close to them.

## RESOURCES THAT FACILITATE THE MELTDOWN PROCESS

*I Know I Made It Happen,* by Lynn Blackburn (1991), is a book that recognizes and addresses children's *magical thinking and subsequent guilt* that they are in some way responsible for the loss of a loved one. Children and adults can use this book as a resource with which to identify and relate. It is about the many things children feel they may have caused.

As I read this book to kids experiencing a great loss in their lives, they often look at me and say that they can relate to the story. Robert explained, "It's my fault my dad died. If only I had not been playing at my baseball game and been with my dad at his baseball game when he had his heart attack, I know I could have saved him." "I killed my mother," insisted Margaret. "How did you do that?" I asked. "Well," she said knowingly, "she picked me up the night she had her heart attack and, if she hadn't done that, she wouldn't have died."

We then began to talk about the *facts* of heart disease and separate these facts from children's magical thinking. They began to meltdown an important, frozen block of time. The unbearable responsiblity of not saving their parent from death was brought out into the open, and the new understanding that it was not their fault that their mom or dad died was allowed to be created.

*Aarvy Aardvark Finds Hope* (1988), by Donna O'Toole, is a story to be read aloud to young children. O'Toole uses animals as a vehicle for understanding the journey of grief and uses storytelling as a device to allow readers of any age to identify with their own pain and subsequent healing. Aarvy grieves over the sudden loss of his mother and brother who were taken away to the zoo. Aarvy had felt abandoned by his dad in the same way when he was a baby. These multiple losses and the shock of each loss creates a story of complicated grief that even a young child can understand and identify with.

*Aarvy Aardvark Finds Hope* (the video), by O'Toole (1994), presents puppets and visual imagery to allow the story to come alive for young people. The pace of the film is designed to allow kids to feel a sense of the slow moving process of grief itself.

*The Hurt* (1983), by Teddi Doleski, is a wonderful book with which to open discussion of painful feelings for children and adults of all ages. It is a wonderfully simple story with an underlying universal theme: *When we lock in our hurts, we become lonely, isolated, and scared.*

## ACTIVITIES TO HELP YOUNG CHILDREN WITH COMPLICATED GRIEF

■ Read stories to children that allow them to project their feelings onto the story characters. This opens a dialogue with a child in a way that is not threatening.

■ Allow children to visualize their hurt, fear, or pain. They then can draw, make use of clay, or imagine these symbolic feelings being able to talk. If the hurt could talk, 8-year-old Nancy explained, it would say "Why me?" Nancy had experienced multiple losses, including the death of her younger sister. Feelings of having bad luck or being punished began to emerge.

■ Invite children to make a loss time line, filling it in with people and dates in chronological order according to when people died. This loss time line becomes a concrete representation of all the losses one has experienced.

■ Create with children a geneogram or family tree using a circle and square to represent those people still living and those people who have died. Kids can see not only the extent of the losses they have had but also the support system of people that are remaining.

 By helping children put their feelings outside of themselves, we can facilitate their healing. Sharing feelings diminishes the hurt.

## *TOMMY*: A TOOL FOR TEENAGERS

The rock opera *Tommy* is an excellent medium to use in grief work with teenagers. The drama allows the audience to visualize and conceptualize through dance, music, and story the very poignant story of Tommy and his journey through complicated grief. The audience can experience Tommy's pain and actually see his frozen blocks of time appear, continue, and compound themselves through each of his life's traumas. Teenagers who may not relate to material geared to younger children may relate more easily to *Tommy* and the music of Pete Townshend and The Who.

The story begins with 4-year-old Tommy witnessing an all too common occurrance in today's world. His father comes home to find his wife with her new boyfriend. An argument erupts, and Tommy witnesses his father shooting and killing the boyfriend.

Realizing that Tommy witnessed this homicide, his parents immediately begin shouting at him a message over and over again: "You didn't see it, you didn't hear it. You didn't see it, you didn't hear it." As they continue to scream these words, the turmoil and confusion of the police investigation and trial whirl by Tommy.

Tommy stops seeing, hearing, and speaking. He becomes frozen in time. The *trauma of violence* coupled with the *prison of family secrets* still his being. Gazing at his reflection in the mirror is the only way that he can see the child within who remains suspended in time.

At age 10, Tommy is sexually abused by a drunken uncle. Tommy tells no one. Another frozen block of time is created, and he again sees its reflection in the mirror.

A few years later, Tommy is tormented by the neighborhood baby-sitter. *Physically and verbally abused* by him, Tommy again remains still in his silent world, except for the inner voice directing him toward the ever-present reflection of himself in the mirror. He sings to this reflection, "See me, feel me, touch me, heal me," throughout the play—his ongoing attempt to melt his own frozen blocks of time and be free.

Tommy's mother's frustration with his *silence* ultimately leads her to smash his mirror in a fit of rage. At this moment, the audience gets to see the 4-year-old, 10-year-old, and 17-year-old parts of Tommy, thus far held prisoner by trauma. The parts stand separately on stage. This visual representation shows the complicated grief Tommy held at various ages and how these parts needed to be brought together, out in the open, in order for Tommy to heal.

Tommy becomes a pinball wizard and a rock star. His fame brings him many followers who look to him to find the way to their own happiness. His message to them is to look within themselves, for the answers are buried deep within each one of us.

Tommy's story is very uplifting. We see his silent struggle with pain and his eventual breakthrough to become conscious of his tragedy. Through his inner wisdom and insight, he can show teenagers a way to reframe their own private hurts and explore traumatic memories. This self-knowledge constitues a rite of passage with which young people can identify.

# HOW TO HELP TEENAGERS COPE WITH COMPLICATED GRIEF

## Journals

*Fire in My Heart, Ice in My Veins,* by Enid Traisman (1992), is an excellent interactive journal available for teenagers. It provides many resourceful ways for teens to put their thoughts and feelings on paper.

## Manual

*Teen Age Grief* (TAG), by Linda Cunningham (1990), is an excellent manual for initiating and facilitating grief support groups for teens. Kids explain how they grieve and provide practical ideas that may help others in their process.

## Music

Music is a powerful form of communicating, especially for teenagers. Not only can music be an excellent vehicle for bringing feelings and memories to the surface, but it also provides a way to help kids relax. Teenagers can be asked to share music that reminds them of their loved one or a favorite song that their loved one liked. If they play a musical instrument, they can bring it to play the musical selection. The following music may be highly effective with teenagers.

"Memories" sung by Barbra Streisand
"I'll Be There" sung by The Escape Club
"Tears in Heaven" by Eric Clapton
"I Always Thought I'd See You Again" by James Taylor
"It's So Hard to Say Good-bye to Yesterday" by Boyz II Men
"Children Will Listen" sung by Barbra Streisand
"That's What Friends Are For" sung by Whitney Houston

## Books

In *Death Is Hard to Live With,* by Janet Bode (1993), teenagers openly express how they have coped with the loss of someone they have loved.  These losses include death by suicide and homicide.

*The C-Word*, by Elena Dorfman (1994), is a book for teenagers and their families coping with the disease of cancer and the deaths it may cause.

*When a Friend Dies*, by Marilyn Gootman (1994), is a book for teens about grieving and healing.  Gootman uses the words of many teens, affirms their feelings, and presents positive ways of coping with these feelings.

*Facing Change*, by Donna O'Toole (1995), provides an abundance of information and coping choices to assist the grief process for teens.  Practical ways to help normalize grief are included.

## WORDS TO USE WITH COMPLICATED GRIEF

**Abuse:** Abuse is when someone hurts someone else's body or feelings over and over and over again and usually knows he or she is doing it. Sometimes someone can hurt us just one time, and that can be abuse too. The hurt can come from screaming, hitting, using mean words, or touching in a way that is uncomfortable or confusing to someone. Not being protected from an adult using a child's body in a sexual way doesn't feel good.

**Casket:** A casket is a special box in which a body is buried.

**Cemetary:** A cemetary is a place where a body in a casket is buried.

**Cremation:** Cremation is burning the dead body until it changes to ashes.

**Death:** Death is when the body stops working (Fox, 1988).

**Depression:** Depression is extreme feelings of sadness that last a long time.

**Funeral:** A funeral is a gathering of friends and family to remember a person who has died, to honor his or her life, and to say good-bye. Usually it is just before the body is buried.

**Grief:** Grief is all the feelings we feel after someone close to us has died. We can feel sad, angry, frightened, or guilty.

**Guilt:** Guilt is a feeling that makes us think we are the cause of something and that we may have done something wrong.

**Homicide:** Homicide is the act of killing someone else so that his or her body stops working. Sometimes people kill out of anger, fear, or just forgetting that every human being is important. There is always another way to work out our feelings without hurting someone else.

**Mourning:** Mourning is the way we take our feelings of grief and do something to remember the person close to us. It is how we show our sorrow.

**Rage:** Rage is a feeling of extreme anger.

**Shame:** Shame is a feeling of extreme guilt.

**Stigma:** Stigma is a mark of shame of someone doing something wrong.

**Suicide:** Suicide is the act of killing yourself so that your body won't work anymore. People do this when they feel there is no other way they can think of to solve their problems, or they may feel at the moment that life is not worth living. People always can get help.

**Terror:** Terror is a feeling of extreme fear.

# PART II
# BREAKING THE SILENCE

# Chapter 2

## BREAKING THE SILENCE ON SUICIDE

■ Secrets ■ Shame ■ Guilt ■ Abandonment

# Whoever Preserves One Life, It Is as If He Preserved an Entire World

*Talmud*

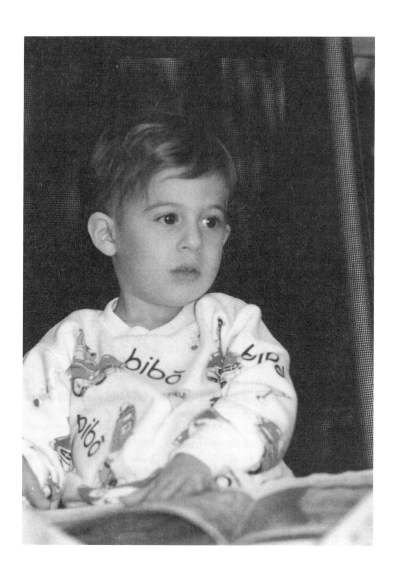

## FACTS ABOUT SUICIDE

It is estimated that each year between 7,000 and 12,000 children in the United States have a parent who commits suicide.

Webb, 1993, p. 137

Suicide is the second leading cause of death for young people between the ages of 15 and 25.

Smith, 1989, Introduction

It is expected that one young person in the United States will commit suicide every 90 minutes.

Smith, 1989, Introduction

## COMPLICATION OF SUICIDE

Alice was a woman whose husband Matt had committed suicide 6 years before she came to see me, when her son Brian was 4. Since then she had not dated and had no desire to be with a man. Her husband had left her a suicide note blaming her for his death. Over and over she repeated stories of abandonment by friends and relatives who stopped calling or seeing her after her husband died. She felt totally rejected by her husband, and these feelings were compounded by rejection from the rest of her world.

## A FROZEN BLOCK OF TIME

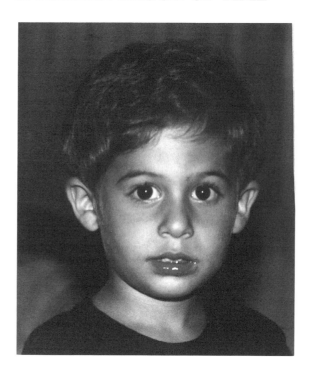

Why, she asked, did her family give so much attention to her sister, Page, whose husband died of cancer, and none to her and her son, Brian? No one ever mentioned her husband or his death. The *loneliness* of her mourning became greater than Matt's death. She could not grieve outwardly. No one would listen. Alice's *guilt and shame* over Matt's suicide grew. With no other adult to share it with, it became their unspoken family secret. Alice *isolated* herself and her son. She allowed no men into her life.

During Brian's routine 10-year-old checkup, the pediatrician suggested that Alice receive grief counseling. The doctor also stressed that Brian might need to begin having some male figures in his life. Since his dad's death, Brian's mom and he had spent much of their time only with each other, without any other masculine role models for Brian to identify with. Sometimes children feel different if they don't have a dad around.

Shown here is a picture Brian drew. His Uncle Tom was the central figure. Alice was shocked because Brian rarely saw his uncle. For Brian, the primary problem seemed to be not having a man in his life to spend time with and look up to, and seemed not to be his dad's death by suicide. The issue of how his dad had died had not emerged.

The *complication of suicide* left Brian without a dad. The *complication of suicide* left Alice with fear. Her fear was that speaking about or telling her son about suicide would destroy their lives even more. The terror that another man could destroy them both kept Alice and Brian isolated and alone. Suicide built a powerful wall around their physical and emotional home that no one could penetrate.

This is Mom and Tom watching me on the playground.

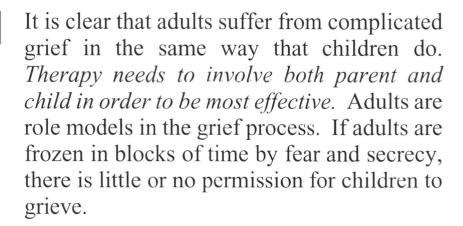

It is clear that adults suffer from complicated grief in the same way that children do. *Therapy needs to involve both parent and child in order to be most effective.* Adults are role models in the grief process. If adults are frozen in blocks of time by fear and secrecy, there is little or no permission for children to grieve.

## SUICIDE—A JOURNEY OF DESPAIR

As a certified grief therapist and grief educator in private practice in Kensington, Maryland, I am confronted more and more with the suicide ideation in children who consider it as a possible solution to solving problems. In my search for literature for children on the topic of suicide, I found only one book, *I Wish I Was in a Lonely Meadow*, created by the Dougy Center in Portland, Oregon. In this book, children who have experienced a suicide in their family tell of their journey.

I have found projective techniques to be extremely effective in working with children and their thoughts and feelings of self-hatred and self-destruction. So often children cannot or will not verbalize their feelings directly. Sometimes their emotional environment reinforces silence. Often there are no role models to demonstrate feeling vocabulary and language. Children may be terrified of telling some deep family secret because of shame or personal threats. We need to help children acknowledge and express those feelings in therapy. Projective techniques such as storytelling, drawings, toys representing people and events, and clay often can open the locked doors to children's underlying and hidden grief.

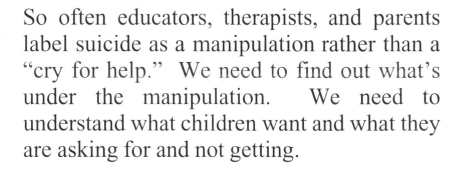

So often educators, therapists, and parents label suicide as a manipulation rather than a "cry for help." We need to find out what's under the manipulation. We need to understand what children want and what they are asking for and not getting.

## COMPLICATED GRIEF: SUICIDE AND MULTIPLE LOSS

Henry was a child who began grief therapy at age 8. His mom brought him to work with me because he was *acting out constantly in school* and had been expelled several times. She relayed his patterns of *sleep difficulty* and occasional *bed-wetting*. The school recommended that Henry get special help.

Henry had experienced multiple losses. Within the past 6 months, his dad had been murdered. Other losses included his parents' previous separation and divorce, his mom's serious illness, which often left him living with Grandmother, and his dad's moving away and subsequent death. Henry was an only child who had *moved at least six times* in his life, often living with his grandmother and five other cousins. His mom, Carol, relayed that Henry had *a history of being disruptive*, walking out of the classroom since kindergarten, and that his rage had grown since his dad's death.

His mom had a new boyfriend who was living with the family. Henry would not talk about the boyfriend directly. Mom went to school at night, leaving Henry with Grandmother or sitters. He usually went to bed very late and had to be at the sitter's at 6:00 a.m. so Mom could go to work. His teachers reported *poor attention in school* and *outbursts of aggressiveness and rage* toward teachers and classmates. He had *difficulty concentrating,* and his grades were poor. Yet he loved attention and could be a very helpful and pleasant child.

We began by establishing rapport. We read stories and played games. We decided to make a contract about his behavior and what we would agree to do. Many times we role-played and, on one occasion, Henry wanted to take the part of his father. I was Henry. As he began to pretend he was his dad, he started screaming out, "I'll beat you with an electric cord. Call the cops! Put you in jail!" The next week Henry came in and told me that if anyone talked about his dad, Henry would get angry enough to "throw a desk out of the window and burn down the school."

Other times Henry came in and didn't speak. One day he began drawing pictures of a genie. I asked what he would wish for. His answer was, "I wish I was free."

___

## HENRY'S SYMPTOMS OF COMPLICATED GRIEF

- Bed-wetting
- Difficulty sleeping
- Headaches
- Inability to concentrate
- Poor grades
- Outbursts of aggressiveness and rage
- Impulsivity in leaving class
- History of previous multiple losses
- Conflicted relationship with deceased
- Sudden death of father

## MELTDOWN PROCESS: WORKING WITH ANGER

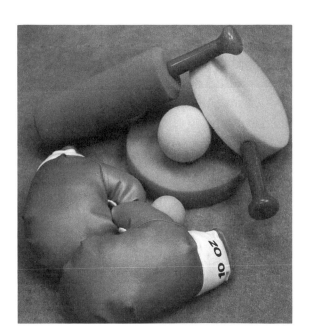

1. Use a punching bag, gloves, or foam bats. Draw or name the person the child is angry with or a feeling the child has toward that person and put it on the punching bag.

2. Tear up old magazines and throw pieces around the room.

3. Punch a pillow.

4. Scream into a tape recorder or paper bag.

5. Write a furious letter. Rip it to pieces.

6. Pound clay. Make a person the child is angry with and create a dialogue or destroy the figure.

7. Use puppets to role-play an angry scene.

8. Call on a telephone and tell the person your angry feelings.

9. Do physical exercise to release some of the angry energy (run, jump rope, play ball, etc).

10. When possible, tell the person directly when you are angry. "I'm angry at you for yelling at me when I spilled my milk."

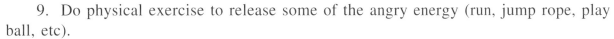

### SUGGESTIONS FOR MOM TO HELP HENRY

■ Choose an activity such as karate or another form of exercise to help Henry work with some of his anger energy. He also can yell in the shower or go outside and shout if he needs to.

■ Read the story *Don't Pop Your Cork on Monday* (Moser, 1988) with Henry to help work with some stress techniques.

■ Read the story *I'm Mad* (Crary, 1992) with Henry to find possible alternatives to hurting others with anger.

■ Get professional evaluation by psychiatrist for possible medication for depression and/or attention deficit.

■ Suggest a team conference at Henry's school to request a complete evaluation with the possibility of special placement to meet his specific needs.

■ Communicate with teacher and counselor often.

Henry continued to display extreme emotionality and an inability to control his feelings. Henry's walking out of the classroom and refusing to come back and displaying frequent emotional outbursts led to his expulsion from school. One day Henry left school and threatened to jump off the roof. School personnel immediately sent him to the emergency room of a nearby hospital where he was evaluated; the medical staff urged a reevaluation of the strength of his antidepressant.

Carol called the therapist who was administering Henry's medication at her health insurance program, relaying the seriousness of her son's behavior. She was told that Henry needed to wait 3 weeks to get an appointment. We both called and left messages urging an immediate appointment and received no return calls or replies. The days passed, and we continued to call this company.

Finally we spoke to Henry's doctor who appeared angry that we were insistent on reevaluating the medication. "This child says he doesn't want to live," I reminded her. Her response was that Henry was just being manipulative. "Isn't suicide the ultimate manipulation?" I replied. "You wouldn't want to be responsible for that, would you?" She made an appointment for him the next day.

During the time that Henry expressed feelings of not wanting to live and the beginning of a satisfactory dosage of his antidepressant, we talked openly about his suicidal feelings.

1. I asked Henry *if he thought about killing himself.* He said, yes, he didn't want to live.

2. I asked Henry if he thought about *how he would kill himself.* He replied, "jump off a roof." We talked about how problems may seem so big that there does not seem to be a way out, but there always is.

3. *We made a contract.* Henry and I both signed it. Henry agreed not to hurt himself or anyone else until he saw me again next week. I gave him my telephone number to call as well as his teacher's and guidance counselor's phone numbers if his destructive feelings and thoughts reoccurred. School personnel were consulted and were in agreement with the contract.

---

## HENRY'S CONTRACT

January 10, 1994

I will not hurt myself or threaten to hurt myself until I see Linda in 1 week. If I have these feelings, I will call:

| | |
|---|---|
| Linda | 123-4567 |
| My mom | 123-4567 |
| My teacher | 123-4567 |
| My counselor | 123-4567 |

Signatures:          *Henry*                    *Linda*

I will tell my teacher when I begin to feel angry and frustrated in school and say that I need to see the guidance counselor.

Signatures:          *Henry*                    *Linda*

---

4. We decided on *ways to get help* at school. These included permission for Henry to call Mom at work, call me at work, or leave class to talk to the guidance counselor.

A team conference was held with school personnel, Henry's mother, and myself. There was great concern over his failing grades, his hostility toward others, and his continuing thoughts of not wanting to live. The team's recommendation was for a full battery of diagnostic tests and a careful monitoring of his antidepressant. We were to meet again when the tests were completed.

When Henry's dose of antidepressant was increased, he became withdrawn and quiet. The dose was lessened, and he appeared calmer. Yet he constantly relayed his inner need to be free. When the team met again, there was still great concern that the school was not meeting his needs. He was anxious, fearful, and still wished for a peaceful place. They felt he had stopped learning. When he met failure, he would continue his pattern of shutting down, getting angry, and leaving. The psychologist reported during testing that Henry likened himself to a computer. "You're trying to take everything out of my mind," he explained. She felt he was afraid of being hurt or hurting other people. His behaviors were a desperate cry reflecting his inner feelings of helplessness.

The decision of the team was to provide a resource teacher for Henry as well as home teaching to decrease his hours in school. The school would initiate procedures for special placement services to meet Henry's academic and emotional needs. A small self-contained classroom, individual attention, and ongoing counseling were requested.

Henry is now in a special school placement where he receives daily counseling and a multitude of resources. There are eight children in his class, and his mom recently called to let me know that Henry earned the award for the best kid of the month. Henry is one of the lucky ones. He had support, love, and help in a system that easily could have buried his needs and his wants and his underlying silent screams for help. The use of projective techniques was a valuable tool for me to begin unravelling the knot of despair that lay twisted deep within Henry's soul.

## COMPLICATED GRIEF: SUICIDE AND ITS RELATIONSHIP TO THE GRIEF PROCESS OF THE SURVIVING PARENT

Nine-year-old Justin's mom committed suicide when Justin was 4. Justin's dad, Steve, decided to get help for his son because school personnel were complaining about his continual fights on the playground. When questioned by his dad, Justin said it made him really angry when kids asked him how his mom died. He said he just wanted to hit them and run away. Steve never had told his son the truth. Steve told me that he was unable to do that. A family secret lived in their house and grew as poisonous as any cancer. Justin had been told that his mom died of a heart attack. Further details had been left out.

I usually feel that kids know that they are being lied to, and uncertainty and potential rage become an all-pervasive part of their lives.

We began to discuss what Steve could tell his son about the truth. At first, Steve refused to role-play this dialogue with me. After several weeks, he gained the courage to try. The terror of telling his son and the overwhelming shame of his wife's suicide had silenced Steve's voice for 7 years. We then discussed the possibility of putting these ideas on paper in a letter to Justin. Steve could send it, read it, or discuss it if and when he was ready. The possibility that Justin could hear about the suicide from someone else was brought out into the open. Asking Steve what would happen if Steve were to die suddenly in a car accident was a motivator. Who would tell Justin the truth about his mom? What would Steve want Justin to know?

The letter was a written safeguard of Steve's truth. Writing a letter was also a step for Steve toward being able to externalize his secret. It brought him one step closer to the possibility of talking to Justin about Mom's death.

*Dear Justin,*

*I've been waiting to tell you about Mom's death and how she died. I didn't know how because it is such a difficult and painful subject, but I feel you need to know some things.*

*For a long time Mom was having problems keeping her thinking straight. She would get depressed and scared way beyond the normal way we all sometimes get depressed and scared. She went to a doctor, but he wasn't able to help her very much. The more depressed and scared she got, the more mixed up her thinking became. She was not able to organize her life, she would just not show up at work, she would do strange things like yell at the mailman one day and then the next day forget she ever did that.*

*When Mom wasn't feeling mixed up, she would like to be with you. She would read to you, sing to you, and love to rock you in her arms. She talked a lot about how much she loved you and how scared she was that she was not a good enough mother. I told her she was a good mother but it didn't matter. Her thinking was very mixed up.*

*Eventually she got so mixed up that she began to think that we would be better off without her. The doctor and I told her that was not right, and she even acted like she believed us, but really she didn't believe us. For some reason we don't understand, it was as though she couldn't believe us. She just wasn't thinking straight.*

*One day she took a whole bottle of sleeping pills.  We don't know if she was confused and only meant to take one or two pills or if she meant to take them all, knowing that it could make her body stop working and die. If this was her plan, I feel she did it thinking it was out of kindness and love for us.  If so, that would have been the most mixed up thought she ever had!*

*We don't know all the reasons some people do this.  Sometimes kids may worry that if a parent decides to end their own life, they might too.  Suicide is not catching.  It is not hereditary or genetic.  Mom's depression and decision not to live belonged to her.  You are separate and in no way caused or created it.*

*What we are sure of is that Mom made a mistake.  Maybe she couldn't help it, but it was a mistake nevertheless.  If her mind was working right she would have easily understood that her solution to her problems would create an even bigger problem.  She would have understood that it would fix nothing to end her own life.  She would have realized how much we would miss her because we loved her so much.  And she would have looked harder for another way if only to not cause us so much sadness and pain.  It makes me very angry because I miss her so very much.*

*Justin, Mommy made a very big mistake.  She felt ending her own life was the solution to her problems.  Nobody knows what the right solution might have been, but we would have continued to help her look for it if she would have just given us more time. There's always another way.  It's as if Mom felt trapped in a room with no doors and no windows, except there is always a door, Justin.  She just needed to find the handle to open it.*

*Your mom and I love you very much,*

*Dad*

## WAYS TO TALK WITH CHILDREN ABOUT SUICIDE

- *Define suicide* as when "someone chooses to make his or her body stop working."
- *Give age-appropriate facts* and explanations.
- *Dispel myths* of suicide.
- *Retell good memories.*
- *Model feelings* and thoughts for children.
- *Emphasize that suicide is a mistake* because there "is always another way out."


Writing can be easier than saying, and saying is easier after writing. Steve felt great relief after we finished. He said he still was not ready to tell Justin the facts but felt much more *prepared* for when that time would come. I often feel that when the adult survivor of a suicide is ready to tell a child, the child will be ready too. *Steve was frozen in time with the stigma of suicide.* This first preparatory dialogue with Justin was the beginning of Steve's meltdown process.

*Parents are role models for children.* Children learn much more from watching what we say and do than from what we tell them to say or do. The fears and terrors that stop them from speaking the truth may seem protective but actually inhibit the freedom for children to grieve. Kids need to know the truth, and adults need the words to use to tell them. We, as caring adults, can help provide the words that free families from the bondage of secrecy.

## COMPLICATED GRIEF: SUICIDE AND SHAME (STIGMA)

Jason was a fourth-grader whose dad committed suicide on his birthday, a week before summer vacation. Jason and his cousin were preparing to spend the summer vacation with Jason's dad in Colorado. Jason stopped going to school, afraid to face his peers for fear they would question him about his dad's death. He was too embarrassed to talk about it. He was angry and bored, and much of his summer was spent fighting with his mom and friends. Jason rarely talked about his dad. Fearing he might need to acknowledge *how* his father died, Jason decided not to tell anyone *that* his father died.

Jason was frozen in time. He couldn't grieve for his dad because he wouldn't talk about his dad's death. When school began that fall, Jason said he needed to make new friends, refusing to call friends who didn't know of his dad's death. The fear of explaining *the way* his dad died kept him from explaining *that* his dad died. Remaining ashamed and silent, Jason experienced not only the loss of his dad but of friends as well. Jason's need to separate who the person was from how the person died was essential. We began by talking about suicide. "Suicide means not caring about yourself," Jason explained.

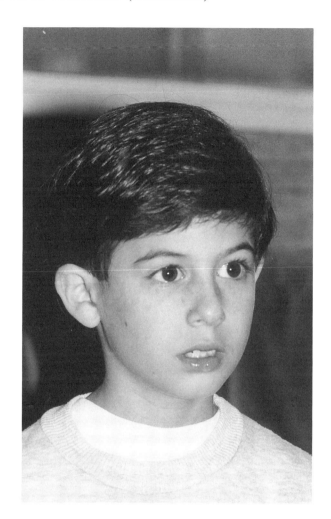

Another child, 12-year-old Dana, also had experienced similar feelings about suicide. Her ideas are revealed in the following explanation that she wrote.

## Suicide

The Way I see it is that everyone who has died, exept for elders, committed suicide.

### — Examples —

1. heart attack - overweight smoking (did nothing about it)

2. hit by car - didn't look both ways before crossing the street.

3. Murdered - Was probably involved with some people who were killers.

4. Cancer - Smoking - Never quit

Defenition of Suicide -
    Everyone does it sooner or later. (Hurt themsleves out of carelessness)
                                    Dana

## COMPLICATED GRIEF:  SUICIDE AND ABUSE

When Ashley was 10, her dad Peter committed suicide.  Before his death, Peter had been emotionally abusive to Ashley and her mom.  His behavior had been erratic and unpredictable, and Ashley and her mom lived in constant fear of his actions.  When he died, secretly Ashley felt *great relief* and *immense guilt* about feeling that way.  Her feelings of relief and safety could not be reconciled with her grief.

When kids have been abused by a parent, and then the parent dies, many ambivalent feelings surface.  Once free from the fear of abuse, overriding guilt can appear. This guilt freezes children in time and buries the normal grief feelings for the death of the abusive parent.

A seemingly unrelated incident became a trigger in releasing a frozen block of time for Ashley.  Ashley had heard at school that a dog had gotten killed. She came home furious at her dad for giving her dog, Misty, away when Ashley was 5.  She remembered the day well.  Her father had decided for no apparent or logical reason that he didn't want Misty because she had begun to bark.  He put the dog on a leash, took her in the car, came back without her, and never said what he did with Misty.

No one ever saw Misty again. This action sent a powerful message to Ashley. If Dad didn't like something she did, what would he do to her? Dad's suicide felt like Misty's story of abandonment. Dad left one day, for no apparent or logical reason to her, and never came back. He took his life and didn't say why.

Remembering and acknowledging Misty's abandonment put Ashley in touch with her rage about it. Only then could she begin to grieve for her dad. She felt validated by caring adults who gave her permission to express her anger at her father and to express the terror she inwardly held that she too could be abandoned. Knowing that it was okay to have those feelings that were very natural under the circumstances enabled a healthier part of Ashley to emerge.

Often adults admonish children by stressing, "You shouldn't feel like that. Your dad is dead. Don't talk about the dead." Sometimes kids internalize the suicide, the homicide, the violence, or the abuse and feel that they are that act and carry inside of them that shame of how the person died or how they themselves were mistreated. Children can begin to feel free when they realize that they are not responsible for any act that their parent or loved one has committed.

## SUICIDAL THOUGHTS IN CHILDREN

Sometimes kids have suicidal thoughts and ideas and *are afraid to express them*.

Sometimes kids have suicidal thoughts and ideas and do express them and *no one listens*.

Sometimes kids have suicidal thoughts and ideas, and they are *accused of being manipulative*.

Sometimes kids feel they *don't want to live anymore* because they feel there is no way out of their problems.

Sometimes we as caring adults can help by just *providing a space* where they can say, "I feel I just don't want to live anymore."

The following drawings illustrate the emotional pain a child felt after experiencing the sudden death of his older brother, Adam. Tony was 7 when Adam overdosed on drugs.

As hard as it is for us as caring adults to see and hear Tony's feelings of agony, we can only imagine how much harder it would be for this child to live with these feelings in silence.

This is me and this is my soul.
The pain is in the center of my soul.
It's kind of like a disease.
Sometimes I feel like killing myself so I'll disappear and not have pain.

Tony was having suicidal thoughts that were increasing as the anger and frustration over his brother's death in his family grew. Tony's parents were enraged after Adam's death, and arguments escalated between them, with Tony feeling like he was in the middle.

Tony expressed his pain in his drawing. "I feel the walls are closing in on me. I can't stand it anymore," he shouted as he drew his picture. "Who are the walls?" I asked. "My parents," he replied.

## SIGNS OF SUICIDAL FEELINGS

1. **Depressing thoughts and feelings** over the loss of a loved one causing prolonged grief. The child may wish to join a parent who has died.

Child may say, **"I wish I was dead too."**

2. **Wishing to punish the person** who died or left or making threats of getting even.

Child may say, **"Dad will be sorry he ever punished me. I'll show him."**

3. **Attempting to regain power** or control.

Child may say, **"You can't leave me; I'm leaving you."**

4. **Wishing to die to relieve tremendous guilt** of perception of having done something very wrong.

Child may say, **"I can't forgive myself for Mom's death. I know I caused it. I was so mean to her the night before she died. I must die too."**

5. Exhibiting **self-anger and self-hatred**—angry feelings that cannot be expressed at an abusive parent.

Child may say, **"I hate myself. I don't deserve to live. I deserve to die."**

6. **Crying out for help** as a desperate attempt to relieve overwhelming feelings of frustration and confusion over family conflicts or life events.

Child may say, **"I can't go on. I don't see a way out. It's hopeless."**

7. **Flirting with death** as a game can create a rewarding reaction from peers.

Child may say, **"I dare you to drag race at 100 miles per hour."**

8. **Losing touch with reality** and no longer distinguishing between fact and fiction.

Child may say, **"I'm going to jump off this building and fly."**

9. **Being preoccupied with death**, such as teenagers who plan their own funerals or begin giving belongings away.

Child may say, **"I'd like roses at my funeral. I'm giving all of my jewelry to my friend, Pam."**

10. **Becoming socially isolated.** Child will not socialize and only wants to be alone for sustained periods of time.

Child may say, **"I have no friends. No one likes me or wants to be with me. What's the use?"**

Adapted from MacLean, 1990

## HOW CAN WE HELP CHILDREN WITH THE ISSUE OF SUICIDE?

**Activities**

1.  Make a *memory book* of the person who died.  Include the following:

"Why did you take your life?"
"I feel _____ about how you died."
"If I could do one thing over, what would it be?"

Remind the children that the suicide was not their fault.

2.  Make a *mural* of (a) before death, (b) at the death, (c) at the funeral, (d) after death, and (e) now.

3.  Make a *collage* of healthy ways to work through painful and overwhelming feelings.

4.  Use *third person in language*.  It is less threatening to kids.  "Many people feel . . ." enables children to open up more easily.

5.  Use activities involving *writing, drawing, or talking about secrets*.

*"Secret Witchy"* is a stuffed toy with an opening in her mouth in which kids can put their secrets.

*Secret markers* hide writing until rewritten with encoding marker.

*Lemon juice* with a paint brush hides secret until the message is put under a light.

*Tape recorder talk* is a time when children can whisper their secrets into a tape recorder and play it back only if they choose to share them.

*Computer programs* are useful for storytelling and writing secrets.  "Kid Works" (Davidson & Associates Inc., P.O. Box 2961, Torrance, CA 90509, 1-800-556-6141) is a storytelling program.  The computer will read the story aloud once it is written.

6. *Write a letter* to the person who has committed suicide.  Let the person know how you feel about his or her taking of his or her own life.

7.  Provide a *worry box* where children can place any written or drawn worries about suicide.

 Remind children that they can share their secrets only if they wish. They don't have to. This way they still get to put their secrets outside of themselves and place them on paper.

**Books**

*I Wish I Was in a Lonely Meadow,* by the Dougy Center (1990), is a compilation of children's feelings and experiences of having suicide affect their lives.

*Hurting Yourself,* by Jeanne Harper (1993), is a pamphlet for teenagers and young adults who have attempted suicide or intentionally injured themselves.

**Resources**

Suicide Information and Education Center (SIEC)
201, 1615 - 10th Avenue, SW
Calgary, Alberta
Canada T3C 0J7
403-245-3900

Suicide Prevention Center, Inc.
P.O. Box 1393
Dayton, OH 45401-1393
513-297-9096

 **SUICIDE HOTLINE**
**1-800-621-4000**

## WORDS TO USE WITH SUICIDE

**Death:**   Death is when a person's body stops working.

**Suicide:** Suicide is the act of killing yourself so that your body won't work anymore.  People do this when they feel there is no other way they can think of to solve their problems, or they may feel at the moment that life is not worth living.  People always can get help.

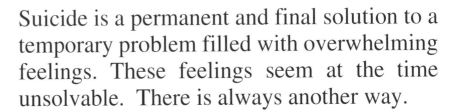 Suicide is a permanent and final solution to a temporary problem filled with overwhelming feelings.  These feelings seem at the time unsolvable.  There is always another way.

## A SUICIDE SUMMARY

### Tell kids to . . .

Talk about it. Tell someone. If someone doesn't listen, tell someone else.

Write, draw, or create ways to take thoughts and feelings and get them outside yourself.

Get help! Go to parents, teachers, counselors, or a trusted adult friend.

### Tell caring adults to . . .

Ask child if he or she has suicidal thoughts.

Ask if the child has thought of ways to kill himself or herself.

Make a signed contract with the child not to hurt himself or herself. Provide names and numbers of people the child can call.

Get professional help.

# Chapter 3

## BREAKING THE SILENCE ON AIDS

■ Worry ■ Fear ■ Shame ■ Secrecy
■ Isolation ■ Rejection ■ Death

Be careful what you say,
children will listen.

Be careful what you do,
*children will see and learn.*

*Stephen Sondheim*

## FACTS ABOUT AIDS

In the United States, 1,500 to 2,000 children who have been infected with HIV are being born each year.

Wiener, Fair, & Pizzo, 1993, p. 85

As of June 1995, over 6,611 children under age 13 and over 2,194 adolescents in this country had been diagnosed as having AIDS (Acquired Immunodeficiency Syndrome).

Centers for Disease Control and Prevention, 1995, pp. 12–14

Estimates are that by the year 1996, 45,600 children and adolescents will have been orphaned by the acquired immunodeficiency syndrome (AIDS) epidemic.

Fanos & Wiener, 1994, p. 43

Forty-two percent of the youths polled between the ages of 9 and 17 reported their greatest worry about their future was contracting the AIDS virus.

Yankelovich Youth Monitor, 1994, p. 50

## DEFINE AIDS FOR CHILDREN

AIDS stands for Acquired Immune Deficiency Syndrome

David Fassler, in his book *What's a Virus Anyway?* (1990), defined AIDS as follows:

 *Acquired* means the disease was caught after the person was exposed to the virus.

*Immune Deficiency* means that the person doesn't have enough white blood cells to fight off infections.

*Syndrome* means a person who has AIDS has a lot of sick feelings and symptoms.

Fassler, 1990, p. 29

Talk to kids about AIDS in simple and clear language. Explain that AIDS is a very serious illness and that is hard for people to get unless they are having sex or using intravenous drugs. Begin by discussing viruses. Explain that AIDS is caused by the HIV virus and that lots of different people can get AIDS. Help children understand that there is much fear and shame surrounding this disease.

---

If I needed to talk to a child about AIDS, the following are the words I might use:

*A **virus** is a germ that can make you sick because it can attack healthy cells in your body. A cold virus can make you sneeze, and a stomach virus can make you nauseous. Most of the time our white blood cells can fight off these viruses and keep us healthy. AIDS is caused by the HIV virus. You can't catch HIV. You can acquire it through blood. The HIV virus **attacks our white blood cells** and kills them. Once this happens, a person can get very sick and die.*

*All different kinds of people get AIDS—moms and dads, teachers, drug users, kids, and even babies. When people have AIDS, they often feel sick. They may feel sad and angry about it too. It's hard for them because sometimes they worry if people will be afraid of them and not want to be their friends. Sometimes people who have AIDS get fired from their jobs. Kids used to get kicked out of school for AIDS, but as people learn more about the disease, this happens much less. This is too bad because people shouldn't treat a person with AIDS this way. Doctors are working to find a cure for*

*AIDS. So far they haven't found one. They do have medicines that may help people with AIDS live longer.*

*People can get AIDS from **having sex** with someone who has the HIV virus, by taking drugs and **sharing needles**, and when **getting blood** from a person who has the HIV virus. If moms have AIDS, sometimes their babies may get AIDS too.*

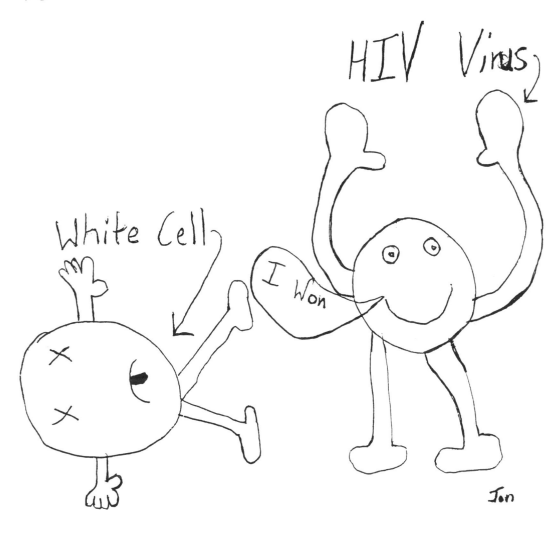

The TV show *60 Minutes* had a recent segment on a summer camp especially designed for and used by children with AIDS and their families. The director of this camp hoped to create an environment that was "not as terrified or angry" as the world from which most of these AIDS patients have come. A little girl at the camp was interviewed and was asked the following question: "Are any kids afraid of you at your school because you have AIDS?" "They don't know," she replied. "Do you feel like you have a secret?" the interviewer asked. "I've always had a secret," she responded, "because my friends would say 'I won't touch you' if they knew I had AIDS."

## CHILDREN WORRY ABOUT AIDS

Melissa *worries* about her family. Her mom and sister have AIDS, and Melissa *wonders what will happen to her family.* She also *regrets the need to lie* about the disease and wishes she could tell the truth. The lies about AIDS feel like "a monkey on [her] back." The following is her way of expressing these feelings. Since the time Melissa wrote this story, her sister has died.

Melissa, age 13

### The Monkey on My Back

I often wonder what will happen to my family because of AIDS. I wish my sister would be all right, but I know she may not be. I wish my mother would start relaxing and not jump to conclusions about my sister so quickly. I also wish my mother will continue to feel well.

I also wish I did not have to lie about my sister's and mother's health. Lying is hard to keep straight, and I wish I could just tell the truth and get the monkey off my back.

Beth worries too. She *worries about dying* because she has AIDS, and she *worries about when and where she will die.* She also *worries about parents and friends cryin*g all the time, and *what will happen to everything she owns.* She's glad she can talk about these things, knowing how hard it is for other people to listen. Here is what she has to say.

(Essays by Beth and Melissa are from *Be a Friend: Children Who Live with HIV Speak*, compiled by Lori S. Wiener, Ph.D., Aprille Best, & Philip A. Pizzo, M.D. Copyright © 1994 by Albert Whitman & Company. All rights reserved. Used by permission.)

## Living with Knowing You Can Die

Everyone knows that you can die from HIV, but no one knows when. Also, no one knows how difficult this is to live with unless you actually have HIV yourself or you love someone with HIV. Living with HIV and knowing that you can die from it is scary. Knowing that you can die is very frightening. I think it is hardest in this order:

Not knowing when this will happen.

Not knowing where it will happen. (I would rather die at home.)

Worrying about my family. For example, will my mother and father ever stop crying? (I don't want them to cry but always remember me riding my pony and being happy.)

What will happen to my stuff and my room? (Casey will probably get most of it, but making a museum would not be such a bad idea.)

Thinking about what my friends will think.

Thinking about dying is hard, but it is good to do because you think about it anyway. Most people don't want to talk about this because it makes them sad, but once you do, you can talk about it more easily the next time. Then you can go on LIVING!

Beth, age 12

## SIBLINGS WORRY ABOUT AIDS

Siblings worry too. Kevin was a 2 ½-year-old foster child who died of AIDS. His older sisters, Miriam and Amber-Naomi, worried about him during his illness, his dying, and even after his death. He died in his mother's arms, surrounded by his favorite stuffed animals with a lullaby tape in the background.

Kevin's mom, Alex, said his 4 ½-year-old sister, Miriam, often worried that she would forget Kevin, and that frightened her. Memories were kept alive through photographs, sharing times spent together, and engaging children in art activities to help remember. Collages about Kevin were made with pictures that told all the special things about him. Miriam also wondered where Kevin went after he died. Alex asked Miriam to draw where Kevin was. She drew the picture shown on this page. She said it was Kevin meeting God and the angels. Miriam explained, "I'm really sad, but God is happy because he has medicine for Kevin. He doesn't have to suffer anymore."

## YOU CAN'T GET AIDS OR HIV FROM . . .

- Touching or hugging
- Toilet seats
- Mosquito bites
- Hair cuts
- Coughing or sneezing
- Sleeping, sitting next to someone, or touching clothes
- Being a friend
- Shaking hands or holding hands
- Donating blood
- Taking care of pets
- Eating, drinking
- Swimming in same pool
- Needles at the doctor's office
- Playing with someone and sharing toys

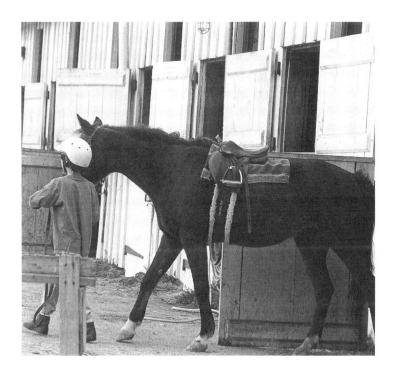

## HOW CAN WE HELP CHILDREN WITH THE ISSUE OF AIDS?

### Activities

Make an *AIDS Feeling Book* with children about their person with AIDS. Here are some ideas:

1. Write and draw about the five most special things you love about your person who has AIDS. What would you like to do to help that person?

Sometimes kids feel helpless when someone they love has AIDS. It helps to draw or write what they love about the person and how they would like to help.

2. Write about what worries you most about AIDS.

Some kids worry about getting AIDS or worry if someone they love has AIDS. If we write down our worries, they usually don't seem so big and scary.

3. Do you have any secrets about AIDS? Draw a picture that tells about it.

Sometimes kids have secrets about AIDS. Writing them down or drawing them helps get them into the open. Place secrets in a secret jar and only share if you want to.

### Books

*Be a Friend* (1994), by Lori S. Wiener, Aprille Best, and Philip A. Pizzo, is a wonderful book of writings and drawings by both children with HIV infection and their noninfected siblings. They tell how it feels to live with this disease and how important it is to be a friend.

*Daddy and Me* (1993), photographs and words by Jeanne Moutossamy-Ashe, is a photo story of Arthur Ashe and his daughter, Camera. It tells of their journey together with his AIDS illness.

*What's a Virus Anyway?* (1990), by David Fassler, is a kids' book about AIDS. It's especially good for explaining to young children how AIDS is a virus.

*Come Sit by Me* (1990), by Margaret Merrifield, is a book for young children that emphasizes the concerns kids have about AIDS.

## Resources

Resources include physicians, local public health units, and AIDS hotline/committees: 1-800-342-2437 in the United States.

 National
AIDS Hotline
1-800-342-AIDS

## WORDS TO USE WITH AIDS

**Acquired:** Acquired means that the disease was caught after a person was exposed to the AIDS virus.

**AIDS:** AIDS stands for Acquired Immune Deficiency Syndrome. It is caused by a virus called HIV. AIDS is really the last stage of the HIV infection when a person becomes very sick. Before that, there may be few symptoms.

**Disease:** A disease is an illness that can be caused by an infection.

**HIV:** HIV stands for Human Immunodeficiency Virus. It is the virus people get with the illness AIDS.

**Immune Deficiency:** A person who has an immune deficiency does not have enough white blood cells to fight off infections.

**Immune System:** The immune system is the body's healthy protection against illness—our body's army to fight sickness.

**Infection:** Infection is a disease caused by germs.

**Syndrome:** The syndrome is the sick feelings and symptoms people have with AIDS.

**White Blood Cells:** White blood cells are the healthy cells that fight off viruses.

**Virus:** A virus is a tiny germ that can make you sick because it can attack healthy cells in your body.

# Chapter 4

## BREAKING THE SILENCE ON HOMICIDE AND OTHER VIOLENT CRIMES

■ Terror ■ Shock ■ Rage ■ Revenge ■ Stigma

Life is not the way it's supposed to be. It's the way it is. The way you cope with it is what makes the difference.

*Virginia Satir*
Campbell, 1991

## VIOLENCE AND THE MEDIA: THE EFFECT ON CHILDREN

The violence that children face today would have been unfathomable to children of past generations. The media and its constant bombardment of this violence into our homes have become a surrogate parent and extended family to our children—influencing them daily.

When children hear and see an ongoing saga of the search for two missing children and the futility of a mother's painful cries for help, they become involved participants in the nation's vigil. Each day they see and hear on the news the latest report on the whereabouts of the missing children. One morning, the kids wake up and hear on TV that finally the children have been found. They are dead! They've been drowned! They've been murdered by their mother! She claims to have put them in a car, seatbelted them in, and let the car roll into a lake. "How could this be?" was the nation's response. She was their mother.

Not only did this woman fool the media and the adults of this nation, she fooled the children as well. This deception led to the unbelievable—a mother murdering her children.

Soon after this event, my son, Jonathan, was doing his homework. He stopped and looked at me. "Mom," he asked, "would you ever murder me?" A new fear and insecurity were now a part of his psyche. I could not control it or change it. It was now a part of his world and the world of other children.

His friend, Josh, asked his mom the next day another poignant question: "What did these kids do so wrong for the mom to kill them?" He thought that the kids must have done something so wrong for their mom to punish them. "The children didn't do anything wrong," she explained. I wonder if Josh and all the children in the nation really believe that. Violence in families is scary and ongoing, and kids usually feel they are in some way responsible.

The FBI's most recent statistics indicate that in 1992, 662 children under the age of five were murdered. Ernest Allen, president of the National Center for Missing and Exploited Children, estimates that about two-thirds of those victims were killed by one or both of their parents.

Van Biema, 1994, p. 50

## FACTS ABOUT CHILDREN AND VIOLENCE

Jerry Adler (1994, p. 44), in his article, "Kids Growing Up Scared," discussed outside influences affecting children and violence.  The following are statistics Adler reported:

---

### Television Violence

The average child has watched 8,000 television murders and 100,000 acts of violence before finishing elementary school.

American Psychological Association

### Real Violence

One in six youths between the ages of 10 and 17 has seen or knows someone who has been shot.

*Newsweek*, Children's Defense Fund Poll

### Violent Crime

Children under 18 are 244% more likely to be killed by guns than they were in 1986.

FBI Uniform Crime Report

---

Violence has become a consistent theme in the life of American children, and its prevalence in the United States is growing and growing.  Randi Henderson (1995), in his article "Caught in the Crossfire," reported the following startling statistics:

■  A dozen American children a day die of gunshot wounds, reports the Children's Defense Fund.  Between 1984 and 1990, the rate of firearm deaths among black males aged 15 to 19 increased by 300%.  The increase among white males that age was 50%.

■  A survey of 1,000 elementary and high school students in Chicago found that more than 25% had witnessed a homicide, 40% had seen a shooting, and more than 33% had seen a stabbing.

■  The *1994 Kids Count Data Book*, a national and state-by-state effort to track the status of children, shows the juvenile violent crime arrest rate increasing by 50% between 1985 and 1991.

■  According to the National Center for Juvenile Justice, teenagers in this country are more than twice as likely to be victims of violent crime as adults.

■  In a recent Harris poll of 2,500 students, 15% of middle and high school students said they carried guns themselves, 11% said they had been shot at, and 59% said they knew where to get a gun.

A friend told me that in her son's high school there was a boy who had a gun with a "hit list" to kill other students at the school.  The students on the "hit list" were told to stay home from school.  Henderson (1995) quoted Thomas Blagburn as saying:

I don't know of any society in history that had children arming themselves, killing and being killed.

Henderson, 1995, p. 31

Children are dying at the rate of about one child every two hours in gun violence in this nation.  Between 1970 and 1991, about 50,000 of our children were killed by guns. This year we will lose 5,000 more.

Edelman (Ryan, 1994)

A kindergarten student in Washington, DC, came to school with a semiautomatic loaded pistol to show his classmates. The mother was arrested and charged with a misdemeanor for giving access to firearms to a minor. The possible danger of a gun in the hands of a preschooler is enormous and frightening. The lack of safety for the children of America is growing daily.

 The Centers for Disease Control and Prevention predicted that, by the year 2005, firearms will become the leading cause of injury-related death in the United States.

*Morbidity & Mortality Weekly Report*, 1994

## A CHILD'S JOURNEY THROUGH VIOLENT CRIME

The following information was explained to me in a workshop by the Dougy Center in Portland, Oregon. The Dougy Center is a nonprofit organization that works with grieving children.

*When children experience the aftermath of a violent death, their **basic belief system is questioned** and often temporarily shattered. The world no longer appears to be a safe place, and the same question is asked over and over again: "How could this have happened?"*

*Often there is a **tremendous strain on the family**. Each person is feeling powerful grief emotions, making others in the family not available for the children. Kids then can feel alone and isolated.*

*Children are usually in shock after a homicide and certainly miss a crucial need to say goodbye. Often there is no physical body. If there is a body that is **mutilated** and children see it, **this is their last vision** of their loved one. They need to continually re-create the act with words, actions, or projective techniques to take it outside of themselves and separate the act of violence from the person they loved.*

*   ***Guilt and over-responsibility** are often a part of the grief work involved with violent deaths. "It's all my fault! Why didn't I stay home? Why wasn't I there? Why didn't I know?" These thoughts plague children.*

*There is a **stigma** that usually exists with violent deaths. People sometimes associate murder happening to "people who are usually bad or criminals." Kids may **distance** themselves and **cut off support** systems or be cut off or ostracized due to judgments of others, fear, and low self-worth. Ryan said his friend Andrew **wouldn't play with him anymore** after Ryan's dad was shot because Andrew wasn't "allowed to play with the son of a murdered dad." Sam went back to school after his dad was killed in a robbery. His friend Andy asked, "Did your dad really get blown up? Did you see it? How many pieces was he in?"*

*   ***Law enforcement issues create a hidden complication.** The story of the incident is repeated and repeated to the police but not to others. Families often put*

grief "on hold" until the legal process is completed. Not knowing what will happen to the murderer leaves an open wound too painful to touch. Sometimes **publicity** about murders is so invasive that **families retreat and isolate themselves** to avoid public scrutiny or sensationalism.

The last part of the legal journey is the **sentencing** of the perpetrator. No matter what the sentence is, often it **doesn't seem to be enough.** One of the questions that kids may demand an answer to is "How dare those bad guys kill my sister?" Even the maximum sentence does nothing to undo the loss and pain. And, all too often, no perpetrator is ever identified.

The **anger, rage, and revengeful** thoughts and feelings that children have after an awful crime are often very **scary**. Children are taught: **"We shouldn't think these thoughts and, if we do, we shouldn't say them to anyone."** This locks the child into the secretiveness of thoughts and feelings as well as the shame of the event so that an additional conflict for the child is created that must be brought out into the open if the child is going to separate the person who died from the terrible event.

## NORMAL RESPONSES TO HOMICIDE AND OTHER VIOLENT CRIMES

So often I have found that children show similar signs of grief when confronted with violent crimes. Terrified mothers and fathers question the normalcy of their children's thinking and feeling after becoming victimized by such a crime. The following is an example of a situation that is all too common when a homicide occurs:

Mrs. Anderson telephoned for immediate grief counseling for her son, Brian. His girlfriend, Annie, had been shot and killed by Annie's former friend who was angry that Annie had taken her boyfriend away. Brian was a good student and had no history of emotional problems. Now, explained Mrs. Anderson, *he continually talks about death*. He constantly *tells the story* of the murder, over and over again. He *wonders if Annie suffered* and tells his parents he is *visualizing the murder* constantly, over and over in his mind. *Violent thoughts* against the murderer plague his mind. Brian has *recurring wishes to join Annie in death* and is preoccupied with *questions about afterlife*. Brian's mom felt horror at watching her child suffer this unbearable pain, and she was relieved to find out that these are all too common responses to tragic circumstances. Recurring wishes to be dead must be taken seriously and professional help must be obtained.

 The victim of a murder dies once. The survivors of the crime experience the violent act over and over in their minds.

## CHILDREN'S COMMON RESPONSES TO VIOLENT CRIME

1. Concerns about fearing that the person suffered.

2. Horror from repeatedly visualizing the crime in their minds.

3. Constant attempt to tell and retell the story of the crime.

4. Need to reenact the crime through play.

5. Seeking revenge against the murderer.

6. Yearning to join the loved one.

7. Desire to plan one's own funeral, especially for teens.

8. Searching and questioning belief in afterlife.

## SIGNALS OF GRIEF AFTER A VIOLENT CRIME

- fear of death
- fear of being left alone or sleeping alone
- desire to leave school or call home
- a need to be with people who have been through the same experience
- drop in grades
- inability to concentrate
- physical complaints (headaches or stomachaches)
- clingy behavior
- bed-wetting
- nightmares
- fear of sleep

## AMERICA'S KILLING FIELDS

Columbia Broadcasting System (CBS) News presented a powerful documentary, *In the Killing Fields of America* (1995), with Dan Rather, illustrating case studies of children being killed in the U.S. One story was about a 2-year-old girl who was abandoned by a system that lost the paperwork that would have placed her in her grandmother's care. Instead she was placed in a foster care home. Her foster mother kicked her to death.

A teenager was abandoned by his mother and father at a young age and left to survive on the streets. He was enrolled in a special school program and was about to graduate from high school. Teachers and students seemed to love him, felt he was a "really great guy," and thought it was amazing that he remained a nice person given all the disadvantages he had experienced in his childhood. He was shot and killed by his girlfriend's jealous ex-boyfriend. In an interview the fall before his death, he was asked what he was thankful for. His response was, "I'm thankful I made it through the summer alive."

As the show ended, Rather left viewers with the following national dilemma:

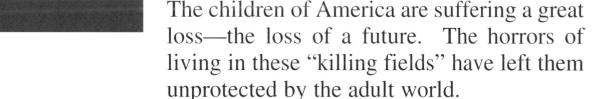

The children of America are suffering a great loss—the loss of a future. The horrors of living in these "killing fields" have left them unprotected by the adult world.

On American Broadcasting Company's (ABC's) Oprah Winfrey special, *There Are No Children Here* (November 28, 1993, Harpo Productions), children living in America's battle-field were interviewed. One child was asked the following question: "What do you see yourself doing in the future? The boy looked back at the camera, nodded, and replied, "I don't see a future."

## WHAT CAN WE DO FOR THE CHILDREN?

### Activities

1. Ask two main questions:

"How did you find out about the death?"
"What do you think happened?"

2. Allow children to draw, paint, write, use clay, or use toy figures; these give them *permission to tell and retell their story.* They then can face the event in the open and see what their minds envision. Usually kids imagine far worse if they have no avenue to project imagined or real conditions. The artwork shown here is an example of a child's perception of the way his dad was murdered as he was driving his delivery truck.

3. Suggest using *dreams:* Children re-create their nightmares through drawing, using clay figures, or playing at a sand table.

4. Have children write new worries and fears and put these inside a *balloon.* Blow up and pop the balloon, and then children can share ideas.

5. Use *paper bag puppets* or other kinds of puppets to act out what happened with a violent death and children's feelings toward the victim and murderer.

6. Have children write a *letter* to the person who was murdered and/or write a letter to the murderer. Make sure children know that the letters will not be mailed.

7. Have children draw in a *memory book,* "One Thing I Wish I Could Do Over." Guilt can create paralyzing secrets.

8. Suggest using *clay* to make someone or something that makes them very angry. Ask, "Why?"

9. Ask children to write or draw the answer to the following question: "If I could be a *magic genie* and give you one wish, what would it be?"

10. Make a *memory wall or mural* to commemorate and tell about the person and how he or she died.

11. Use *pictures from magazines* to create a "feelings" collage or create a story about the death.

## Resources

 National Hotline for Domestic Violence:
1-800-333-SAFE

Explain to children that this number is answered 24 hours a day. The people answering the phone will provide help right away, such as sending police or an ambulance. They may also give the children ideas of other ways to get help.

## Books

*Why Did It Happen?* (1994), by Janice Cohen, was written to help children cope with a violent world. Daniel witnesses a violent crime in the neighborhood and discusses how he feels about it.

*A Family That Fights* (1991), by Sharon Bernstein, is a book that offers words for children and parents to openly discuss domestic violence. It is a story about physical abuse in a family, and the author offers ways to cope with it and get help.

*We Don't Like Remembering Them as a Field of Grass* (Smith, 1991) is a book by children who have had a loved one murdered.

*Just Us* (1993), by Wanda Henry-Jenkins, is a book for teenagers and young adults that defines the journey of survivors of murder victims and how it feels to be so deeply affected by murder.

*Hear My Roar* (1994), by Ty Hochban and Vladyana Krykorka, is a story for young children about a father who becomes abusive to his wife and son. When Mom realizes the effect of this violence, she gets help toward ending the abuse.

*Jessica and the Wolf* (1990), by Ted Lobby, is a story for young children who have bad dreams. This book provides a way to help parents when their children have nightmares.

*Just One Tear* (1992), by K. L. Mahon, is the diary of a 13-year-old who witnesses his father being shot and fatally wounded. His turbulent feelings of being the only witness to the crime and becoming an important person in his father's trial are documented clearly.

# WORDS TO USE WITH VIOLENCE

**Court:** Court is a place where a judge or jury decides how people should be punished if they did something wrong.

**Homicide:** Homicide is the killing of one person by another person—someone choosing to make someone else's body stop working.

**Judge:** A judge is a person who helps decide in a court of law if someone is innocent or guilty of doing something wrong. If the person is guilty, the judge helps decide his or her punishment.

**Justice:** Justice is when a person or court system gives a reward or punishment for something someone has done.

**Jury:** A jury is a group of people who meet in a court to decide if someone is innocent or guilty of doing something wrong. If the person is guilty, a jury or a judge decides how this person should be punished.

**Murder:** Murder is when one person kills another person on purpose.

# Chapter 5

## BREAKING THE SILENCE ON ABUSE

- Guilt ■ Abandonment ■ Pain
- Secrets ■ Shame
- Self-hatred

I never knew grief would feel so much like fear.

*C. S. Lewis* (Campbell, 1991)

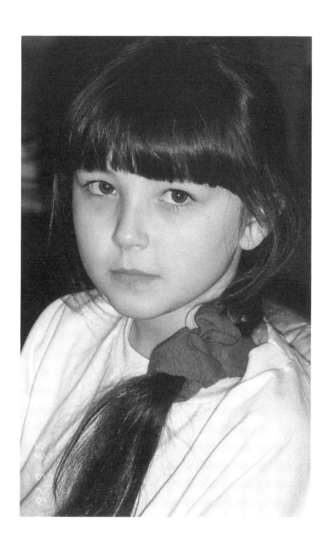

## FACTS ABOUT ABUSE

The estimated number of child abuse victims increased 40% between 1985 and 1991.

> National Committee for the Prevention of Child Abuse, 1994

In 1992, about 1,100 children died from abuse or neglect.

> U.S. Department of Health and Human Services, 1994

Laura MacKenzie, a staff therapist with the sexual abuse unit under Child Protective Services, emphasized a significant increase of sibling abuse among brothers, sisters, and cousins.

In 1991, 3.1 million cases of child abuse and neglect were reported. One child is being abused or neglected on an average of every 10 seconds of the day.

National Coalition for the Prevention of Child Abuse, 1995

Most child abuse reports were made for children under the age of one. The average age of fatalities from child abuse is 2.6.

Child abuse is the leading killer of children under the age of 4.

At least 2,000 children die annually from child abuse, an average of five children dying each day.

Child abuse leaves 18,000 children seriously disabled and another 141,000 children seriously injured each year.

U.S. Advisory Board on Child Abuse and Neglect, 1995

In over 95% of abuse cases, the perpetrator is the child's parent, significant other, relative, friend of family, baby-sitter, sibling, or someone else known to the child.

California Coalition for the Prevention of Child Abuse, 1992

**Abused children feel like ugly ducklings . . .**

**We can help them grow into beautiful swans.**

## REPORTING CHILD ABUSE

Child abuse is against the law and needs to be reported by doctors, educators, therapists, and other caring adults when suspected in order to prevent it and treat it. Kinds of abuse include *physical injury, sexual assault, molestation, and severe emotional abuse.* At least one of the following agencies exists in each state in the U.S.

- Department of Child Protective Services
- Department of Social Services
- Public Social Services Department
- Department of Protective Services
- Social and Rehabilitative Services
- Bureau of Children and Family Services

## EMOTIONAL ABUSE: WORDS HURT—THE STORY OF SAMMY

Sammy was a 9-year-old boy whose father died in a sudden fatal car crash. Sammy and his mom were feeling intense grief, and sometimes this manifested itself in a *rage* over the helplessness of preventing this accident. Sammy often relayed stories of Mom's new *outbursts of anger* since his dad's death. These *misplaced feelings* became targeted toward Sammy.

Sammy came into my office one day asking if he could draw. He began making a giant circle with the word "scream" printed boldly within it. Beneath "scream" was a series of numbers. The following is a representation of his work:

$$8\ 4\ 2\ 0\ 3\ 6\ 7\ 5\ 1\ 7\ 9$$

Sammy explained that the numbers represented his counting to himself while his mother was screaming at him. He said that he would get into the corner of his bed and pull the covers over his head, waiting for the noise to stop.

---

"It feels like my mother hates me," he said. "I get scared and don't know what to do. This is what she says: 'Why do you do these things?' she shouts over and over again." Sammy told me that he felt "too scared to listen, and the yelling was too loud to hear."

---

Sammy and I took the following steps in addressing his grief.

1. I asked Sammy if we could *share his drawings and feelings* with Mom. He agreed.

2. In our next session, we *openly discussed the terror Sammy experienced.* We discussed the roots of this family anger and other ways to work with it.

3. Sammy's *mom agreed to leave the room,* go into another room, and close the door when she felt herself beginning to feel anger she might not be able to control.

4. *Sammy and his mom agreed to meet at a designated time* (15 minutes to 1 hour after the outburst) to discuss without screaming what she was angry about and how Sammy felt about it. Having more control over her anger enabled her to say what she thought and have her son hear her.

5. Sammy and his mom were *encouraged to read together* the book *Hear My Roar* (Hochban & Krykorka, 1994) and use it to create an open-ended discussion.

## EXPLAIN VERBAL ABUSE TO CHILDREN

Help children understand what a verbal assault is and how adults are teaching children through their own behaviors. Adults are role models. On this page, Kevin is learning to model the behavior of his dad. Ask children, "When Dad shouts like this to Kevin, what is Kevin learning to do?"

*"You are a stupid, bad child; I hate you!"*

*"You are a stupid, bad dog; I hate you!"*

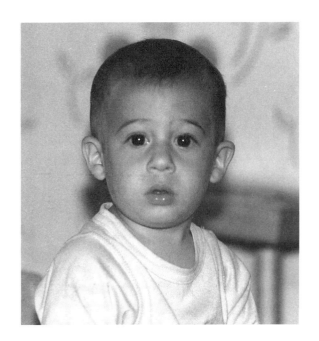

How would Kevin feel?

**small
ashamed
scared
shivery**

What would Kevin prefer to hear?

*"Kevin, when your room is messy, I feel angry. I love you and know you are capable of a good clean-up. I admire your abilities."*

## SEXUAL ABUSE: LOSS OF THE PROTECTION OF THE ADULT WORLD

Alice was a woman who came to my office very disturbed over the loss of her father, the grandfather of her 6-year-old daughter. We began exploring relationships in Alice's life and soon realized that she missed her father so much because in her mind he had been her protector. Alice complained that she *felt unprotected* by her husband and was scared to sleep without her daughter. She worried that they both needed protection.

After many months, we discovered Alice had been sexually molested at age 9. She *blamed herself* for getting into the car with her uncle and told me it was her fault that it happened and how stupid it was of her to have created this. Taken away in a car by this man, her mother's brother, she was sexually abused by him and told that it was her fault and that if she told anyone he would kill her. Alice *remained silent* until she was 40 years old. After the incident, she *became extremely shy and withdrawn, and terrified of being around strangers.* She also *acted out sexually* with her brother, for which she often was punished. From that time on, she *was afraid to go to sleep, having frequent nightmares and fears* throughout childhood.

Alice suffered loss of the innocence of childhood and loss of the protection of the adult world. She carried these losses with her through life with an underlying fear that she never could be protected against the outside world. Alice was frozen in time from a trauma that was so great that she remained silent for 31 years. Holding the childhood terror that she could lose her life if she spoke up about her abuse, she remained unable to relay to anyone what had happened to her. We, as caring adults, need to protect today's children so that other Alices, at age 9, can speak up and be heard.

 ## SIGNS OF ALICE'S GRIEF

- Withdrawal
- Insomnia
- Nightmares
- Fear of strangers
- Acting out sexually
- Self-blame
- Loyalty to abuser
- Difficulty trusting adults
- Hidden or denied feelings

## WAYS TO HELP CHILDREN WITH THE ISSUE OF SEXUAL ABUSE

1. *Know that children cannot always verbalize* an experience of sexual abuse. They may not know the words to use. Doris Sandford (1986), in her book *I Can't Talk About It*, cautioned adults to "be aware of nonverbal cues such as nightmares, withdrawal, school or home behavioral problems, bed-wetting, or unusual knowledge of sexual matters." Some kids may show no physical or emotional signs of abuse.

2. Realize that children usually feel they are the cause of the abuse, and sometimes the abuser tells the child it is the child's fault.

3. Understand that, as Sanford (1986) warned, a child may remain "an emotional prisoner" of the abuse because it becomes difficult to distinguish between sex and love. The abuse creates a blurring of the boundaries, especially when the abuser is a friend or family member.

4. Allow children the opportunity to tell their story over and over again. It is their way of putting it outside themselves.

5. Believe children when they tell you about abuse. Honor their confidence in you and do not repeat the story to someone else while children are present.

6. Tell the child you are sorry this has happened and that you will make every effort to protect him or her.

7. Allow the child to be angry without taking on his or her anger. Adult anger can inhibit the child's expression of feelings.

8. Offer to read books such as *Cat's Got Your Tongue,* by Charles Schaefer (1992), a book about stranger anxiety, or *I Can't Talk About It,* by Doris Sanford (1986), a book about sexual abuse.

Adapted from *I Can't Talk About It* by Doris Sanford, 1986, Portland, OR: Multnomah Press

## ABANDONMENT AND PHYSICAL ABUSE: HAROLD'S CHILDHOOD

Harold was a 10-year-old boy who had continually watched his mom being physically abused by his stepfather, Dan. Harold's biological father had abandoned the family when Harold was 2 and never contacted them again. Harold often talked about his stepfather's violent episodes.

One day Dan had dragged Harold's mother out of the car by her hair, kicked her, and left her by the street as Harold watched. Dan's outbursts of violent rage would erupt toward Harold and his mom, often appearing uncontrollable and unpredictable. Harold lived in terror that he and his mom could be badly hurt or killed.

One particular traumatic memory was of a Sunday afternoon when Dan became enraged for no apparent reason. He took the telephone cord and wrapped it around Harold's neck, trying to strangle him.

Because of many similar experiences, Harold often ran away, staying with friends or relatives and constantly worrying about himself and his mom. He often felt this abuse was his fault and that in some way he was responsible. Sometimes he secretly wished he could kill his stepfather for hurting his mom. He was afraid to tell anyone.

---

## BEING AROUND PHYSICAL ABUSE MADE HAROLD FEEL

- Dirty
- Powerless
- Like running away
- Unprotected

- Like it was his fault
- Worried
- Terrified
- Revengeful

### What Can Harold Do to Get Help?

Harold could help himself in the following ways:

1. Talk to Mom and tell her how terrible it feels when violence happens. Kids need to have people to talk to. Tell other trusted adults such as teachers, grandparents, adult friends, and neighbors.

2. Decide ahead of time on a safe place to go when the violence begins.

3. Ask his parents to get help with counselors or clergy or doctors. Sometimes adults need help controlling their anger.

4. Remember that the violence is not his fault. *The adults are responsible.*

5. Tell Mom to call 911 and get help. If she can't or won't, then Harold can call.

Caring adults could make the following suggestions:

1.  Harold or his mom can call a hotline.  Bernstein (1991) suggested calling the national hotline for domestic abuse: 1-800-333-SAFE.  The person who answers the phone can help Harold and his mom think of ways to get help.
2.  Harold and his mom can stay at a shelter or with a friend or relative.

Adapted from *A Family That Fights* by Sharon Bernstein,
1991, Morton Grove, IL: Albert Whitman & Company

---

## WHAT CAN WE DO FOR THE CHILDREN?

### Secrecy Work

Children feel helpless if they feel they have a secret that they can't share.  If they are holding family secrets that they feel or have been told they cannot talk about, they carry a great burden.  This burden stops normal grief from occurring.  The following words may be useful when said to children before beginning this work.

 "Some secrets are not meant to be kept.  If someone has been hurt or is continuing to be hurt, we can decide together what to do.  Here are some ways we can get the secret out."

1. Encourage children to whisper their secret to a favorite stuffed animal in the room.  Explain that some secrets are meant not to be held or kept.  Decide together if this is a secret to keep or not to keep.

"What is your secret?"
"How do you feel after you have told your secret?"
"Imagine what the stuffed animal might say about the secret."

2. Provide a tape recorder or toy telephone that the children can talk into and tell their secret. If the children use a tape, they can keep it and share their secret when they are ready.

3. Read a story to help children recognize feelings and know that others feel like that too. *Once Upon a Time: Therapeutic Stories,* by Nancy Davis (1990), is an excellent resource of projective stories to help kids free their feelings. Davis is a psychologist with an expertise in working with abused children, their families, and the court system.

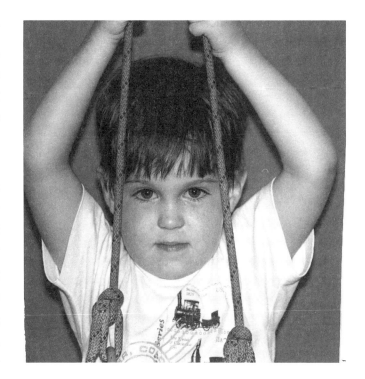

4. Use *computers* as a tool for confidentiality. Today's children are becoming very computer literate, and there are many programs they can use as a silent source of stored thoughts and feelings. Kids can save their work and choose whether to keep it hidden or print it out to share or maintain as a journal. Good examples of computer programs for children are the following:

## KID WORKS

Davidson & Associates
P.O. Box 2961
Torrance, CA 90509

## PSYCH-PIK PROGRAMS

No Secrets Anymore
Feeling Kids
People and Objects
Backdrops

Center for Applied Psychology
Box 61586
King of Prussia, PA 19406

5. *Artwork and poetry* are valuable tools in accessing hidden thoughts and feelings. Children, teenagers, and adults can share present and past memories and perceptions using these vehicles to express their terror and despair.

The drawing shown here is an example about childhood sexual abuse that a little girl continually experienced from ages 3 through 9 by a family member. Her drawings relay her inability to get help, with eyes blindfolded on teachers, doctors, and family members she tried to tell. Only after she got away from the abusive situation could she begin to tell through her artwork and poetry about the painful ordeal she had kept inside.

## THE BRAVEST LITTLE GIRL I KNOW
by Jill

A little girl played with her doll one day
The next, she hugged that doll and said goodbye
Her childhood of colors had faded into gray
And her little heart prayed with screams to die

In a moment she had been drafted into a war
    with shame
And her purity was lost to one that she cherished
He gave her life, yet for this death he was to
    blame
For while her body withstood, her innocence
    perished
An adult was then born, mechanically revived
But that child, has she refused to mature, to
    grow?
She has done both, more importantly, she has
    survived
She lives inside me—the bravest little girl I know

## Resources

American Association for Protecting Children
c/o American Humane Association
63 Inverness Drive, East
Englewood, CO 80112-5117
303-792-9900

Parents Anonymous, National Headquarters
22330 Hawthorne Boulevard
Suite 208
Torrance, CA 90505
1-800-421-0352

Childhelp IOS Foresters
National Child Abuse
P.O. Box 630
Hollywood, CA 90028

 **CHILD ABUSE HOTLINE**
**1-800-4ACHILD**

**TDD FOR HEARING IMPAIRED**
**1-800-2ACHILD**

**THIS IS A 24-HOUR HOTLINE, OPERATING SEVEN DAYS A WEEK IN THE UNITED STATES AND CANADA**

## Books

*Do You Have a Secret?*, by Pamala Russell and Beth Stone (1986), is a book that helps adults talk to children about sexual abuse. It offers important resources for kids who have been victimized.

*Shiloh,* by Phyllis Reynolds Naylor (1991), is a Newberry Medal winning story about a dog that was abused and the boy who loved him.

In *The Words Hurt*, by Chris Loftis (1995), Greg is a young boy whose dad says awful things to him. This verbal abuse makes Greg feel very sad. He finally expresses his feelings to his dad.

*Let's Talk About It,* by Michael Pall and Lois Blackburn Streit (1983), is a book written for kids from 8 to 14 that explains what child abuse and child neglect are in very simple, direct language.

## WORDS TO USE WITH ABUSE

**Abuse:** Abuse is when someone hurts someone else's body or feelings over and over and over again and usually knows he or she is doing it. Sometimes someone can hurt someone else just one time, and that can be abuse, too. The hurt can come from someone screaming, hitting, using mean words, or touching in a way that is uncomfortable or feels confusing. Not being protected from an adult using a child's body in a way he or she does not like or understand can cause bad feelings.

**Bribe:** A bribe is an offer to give a child something he or she wants so that the child will do something he or she does not want to do.

**Guilt:** Guilt is a feeling that makes us think we are the cause of something and that we may have done something wrong.

**Protection:** Protection is being defended or taken care of so that we won't get hurt.

**Rage:** Rage is a feeling of extreme anger.

**Shame:** Shame is a feeling of extreme guilt.

**Stigma:**  Stigma is a label put on someone because others feel he or she has done something wrong.

**Terror:**  Terror is a feeling of extreme fear.

**Violence:** Violence is extreme force or energy used in a physical or emotional way.  It can be sudden and unwanted.

# PART III
# TECHNIQUES

# Chapter 6

# TECHNIQUES FOR COMPLICATED GRIEF

■ Visualization ■ Dreams ■ Silence ■ Puppets ■ Photographs
■ Artwork ■ Clay ■ Toy Figures ■ Punching Bags
■ Tape Recording ■ Storytelling

## CREATE A FEELING OF NORMALCY

Create a feeling of *normalcy* by using *reality checks* when abnormal events and circumstances have happened.

Sharon was a teenager whose dad had been murdered in a drive-by shooting. After going to many therapists who told her on an initial interview that she was clinically depressed and needed medication, Sharon feared that she was "crazy" because of her reactions to unbearable circumstances. "I think I'm going crazy; I'm so preoccupied with death. I'm constantly worried that I'm going to die." I suggested that she receive a medical checkup to help reassure her that she was okay and emphasized to her that children and adults often become overly worried about their health after being directly confronted with death.

Sharon relayed another preoccupation that was worrying her. "I'm terrified the world is going to come to an end." "Your world probably feels like it has come to an end after your dad's death," I responded. She nodded in agreement. Sharon said she felt helpless for not being there to save her dad. The randomness of her dad's killing was both overwhelming and terrifying. His death appeared to be a random act of fate. Understanding that her fears were directly related to her nightmarish experience was the first step in establishing rapport and making the intolerable normal.

**Ways to Help**

Preoccupation with death is a common experience for young children and teenagers after a loved one has died. Kids question what death is, where their loved one has gone, and if something will happen to themselves or surviving loved ones. We can help them with worries and fears by providing "reality checks."

---

1. Provide a visit to the doctor for a checkup to help eliminate some concerns if children begin complaining of physical symptoms.

2. Allow children to call home at a designated time if they feel scared at school and fear for the safety or well-being of a surviving parent.

3. Become familiar with normal grief symptoms. Reassure children that their new fears of death are a normal part of grief and that these fears eventually will subside.

4. Respect the belief systems of children as a foundation for understanding their grief.

5. Invite young children to write about the person who died and any worries, fears, or longings they have toward their loved one. By getting these feelings into the open, we can begin to normalize them.

---

The following is a wonderful example of a loving letter by Amanda, a 15-year-old whose dad had recently died. Their extremely close relationship was a big factor in making this a more complicated grief.

*"My Daddy"*

*My father was a stonecutter—one of those old mysterious trades I will never fully grasp. He was many things in his time. He was a decorator, a teacher, an artist, a painter, things I'll never be. He saw World War II, blackouts, he was almost kidnapped once as a child for being half German. He saw California, he saw Florida, and best yet he saw New Orleans. He saw and did so many things I will never do. He was everything he could have possibly been in his years. He was a lot of things to a lot of people. Never an enemy though, never a tormentor. But most of all, the first thing on the very top of the list, he was mine, he was my Daddy.*

*I used to come home every day after school and immediately rush down to the basement where he would be sitting. Sometimes cutting a stone, or watching television, or drawing, or maybe writing a letter. I was always so glad to see him. I felt as though nothing bad was going to happen to me. I would always hug him, morning, noon, and night. I loved him so much and made sure to tell him all of the time.*

*We always used to make special trips in his little blue car to places all over Maryland and DC. He couldn't walk well, but he could drive just fine. We always had so much fun on those trips. Going down the road with our music blaring over the radio, laughing and chattering about anything we could. We always had somewhere to go, something to do, and always together.*

*To me my Daddy was like no other person in the world. He was bright and shining all of the time. He had fuzzy gray hair, and a fuzzy gray beard, and the most beautiful eyes. He smelled like goose feathered pillows and springtime. He loved me in a way that was mythical and as old as the beginning of time. And I loved him back. He watched out for me, and I watched out for him, every day, every second. We always had time for one another. As long as he was around, I had everything I'd ever need. The only thing he never included me in was his death. And honestly, I'm not so sure that pleases me.*

*Every day when I come home, I still go downstairs just to see if by some chance, some miracle, some grace of God, that he's come back for me. He's come back for me so that we can make this final trip together. I want him to be waiting here for me one of these days when I come home, so he can hug me one last time, so I can feel what it's like to be loved again, so I can feel the roughness of his wool sweater against my face, so I could smell his springtime smell, and most of all so I could go with him this time. If someone were to ask me, do you want to stay here with us in this prison, or go and be free with your Daddy, the choice would be so easy to make. I would go with my Daddy, of course. Even if we had to go through the raging fires of Hell, I would go with him, because we'd be together.*

*But now there are no more stones to cut, there is no little blue car, there are no hugs, there are no hello's, there is no one here waiting for me after school, there is no one here for me to talk to. There is no more love, and there will never again be the feeling of his wool sweater against my face because I wear that sweater now. I wrap it tight around me as I'm waiting for my Daddy. As I'm here leaning against the window sill, I think about how it was all a beautiful dream I once had. So beautiful that I savored every moment of it. But it seems as though the death and destruction pounding on my door woke me up, quickly, without warning. The dream is gone now, and along with it went my Daddy.*

*Amanda  Capps*

Amanda's letter helped her put into words her feelings of hopelessness and despair as well as her great love for her dad. We can feel the pull to join her dad in death, and we can encourage her to pull her dad's love for her into life. Sadness can be reframed into an inner vehicle to propel life. Amanda began to realize that children can carry their parent's love *with* them and in that way, their parent lives on *through* them.

## PROVIDE SYMBOLIC EXPRESSIONS OF COMMEMORATING

Provide *symbolic concrete expressions* of physical, emotional, and intellectual ways of commemorating.

Bonnie and Ken were a couple who experienced the death of their 4-year-old daughter, Lisa, by a drunk driver. The total shock and unreality of never seeing Lisa again created *a physical aching* in Bonnie that could not be filled. The void was excruciating and, as the months went by, deep grief emerged. The grief was compounded by the *lack of someone to nurture* as Bonnie had been accustomed to doing on a daily basis. Winter had turned bitterly cold, and she became plagued by the fear that Lisa would be freezing in the ground and that Bonnie needed to do something to make Lisa feel warm. *Visualizing Lisa in a warm place*

with lots of caring around her was a first step.  Bonnie's belief in an afterlife allowed her to picture her deceased dad (who always had helped keep her warm) being with Lisa.

As Bonnie began to explain her visualization, she said she only saw Lisa in shorts, a tee shirt, or bathing suit  because she had died in the summer, and this clothing was the last visual memory.  Ken remembered that all of Lisa's pictures displayed around the house were taken in the summer.  He wisely suggested *bringing out pictures* of Lisa skiing, bundled up and protected in the winter snow.  We then discussed taking one of Lisa's favorite stuffed animals and dressing it warmly for winter with socks and a warm blanket. Putting this stuffed animal on the sofa by a fire was a soft reminder of the warm love these parents carried for their child and a symbolic gesture of nurturing Lisa.

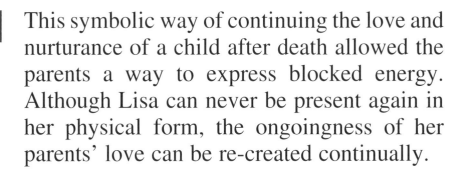

This symbolic way of continuing the love and nurturance of a child after death allowed the parents a way to express blocked energy. Although Lisa can never be present again in her physical form, the ongoingness of her parents' love can be re-created continually.

### Ways to Facilitate Symbolic Projection Through Use of Concrete Objects

Eliana Gil, in her book *The Healing Power of Play* (1991, p. 64), suggested some of the following toys or techniques that work well to encourage children's verbal or play communication.

*Puppet Play.*  Children can use puppets to act out secrets or hidden feelings without identifying these thoughts and feelings as being their own.  Having the children perform puppet work behind a barrier allows them to feel they are hidden and safe when they speak.

*Telephones.* Children can have private role-playing conversations on the telephone.

*Nursing Bottles, Dishes and Utensils, Dollhouses, and Doll Play.* Children can use these concrete props to stimulate expression of hidden thoughts and feelings in a safe way.

*Feeling Cards.* Cards that have illustrations of faces expressing different feelings are useful tools to help a child project storytelling or the child's own feelings or feelings of those close to him or her.

*Sand Play.* Children usually love to use sand. They like how it feels—often it produces a calming effect. Symbolic figures can be used in sand play to create a story, reenact a funeral or other event, or show perceptions of how a loved one died.

*Sunglasses.* Sunglasses can feel magical to children. Sometimes children believe that they can disappear when they are wearing glasses, and no one will be able to see them. If children feel shy or ashamed, sunglasses help them feel they will go unnoticed and then can communicate in an easier way.

## EXPLORE DREAMS

*Dreams* can be used to help children release repressed feelings.

Michelle was a 7-year-old whose mom was killed instantly in a single car collision. Michelle, her dad, and her brother remained stunned by this unbelievable and unimaginable event. *Mom would never come home again*—a reality so great and difficult for children and adults to absorb that it must begin to be bitten off one tiny piece at a time.

Michelle began grief therapy, sometimes talking of her mom, sometimes just needing the physical presence of mothering energy. She wanted to be read to and played with. The need to be nurtured in this way became an important part of our relationship. We cannot expect or demand that children express their feelings directly. They often cannot verbalize their need for the care that has been taken away so traumatically.

Dreams sometimes were talked about and, one day, Michelle asked if she could write a story about her dream and draw a picture too. This dream allowed Michelle to receive the nurturing she needed from Mom at night, nurturing that seemed to be missing during the day. The following is Michelle's dream.

---

## MICHELLE'S DREAM

*I had a dream that I was in the woods. A snake came next to me, so I started to run. I was running and running. I came to the creek. I jumped over the creek and kept running. I ran into the woods and guess what I saw. A wolf! I got very scared. I started yelling. Guess who came. Mommy! She saved me.*

*So we went home. She asked me, "Why did you go out there?" "I just felt like it." "I think you should go home and have a nice warm bath and some hot chocolate and then go to sleep. I'll sleep with you if you want," said Mom.*

*"Mom, you are the best Mom in the whole entire world. I love you."*

*The End*

*Michelle*

---

## Ways to Work with Dreams

1.  Dreams can reflect feelings and problems children may have a hard time sharing openly. B. J. Tongue, in his book *The International Book of Family Therapy* (1982), suggested presenting a picture of a girl or boy lying in bed with the dialogue as another tool to facilitate dream work. An example of such technique follows:

> "Here is a picture of a boy named Tom.  He is having an awful nightmare.  He could be a lot like you.   Could you draw a picture of what Tom might be dreaming?"

Children can decide if they would like to share their work with a parent.  This could be an invitation to involve the family in open feelings.

2. Children can retell their dreams in many ways.  They can be asked to *draw their entire dream* or any part of the dream and write down any thoughts they have about it.  Kids also can be invited to *write down their dreams* as if they were happening as the children are writing. This opens many discussions that can lead to discovering similarities between what is happening in the dream and  what is happening in real life.

3. Children also can be given the choice of *changing the ending of the dream* if they did not like it. Mary dreamed she was lost and could not find her way home. Every time she tried a new road, it led to a place she did not know. She woke up frightened and sad. Mary wanted to change the end of the dream to one she liked. She decided to have her mom (who had died a short while ago) meet her on the road. Mary's new dream ended with her mom saying, "Don't worry. You are safe. Let's find the way home together."

4. *Changing events within the dream* offers children inner alternatives and solutions to perceived problems. For example, Peter dreamed he was being attacked by older boys and was running away and looking for a place to hide. He wanted to change the dream. This time he ran into his father. Together, they turned and faced the bullies, and the bullies ran away.

5. *Give each person, animal, or thing in the dream a voice.* Have children write or say what they feel these different parts of the dream would say if the parts would talk. This helps children see that everyone or everything in the dream can be a part of them and part of what they are thinking or feeling.

## USE DRAWING AND STORYTELLING

*Drawing and storytelling* provide symbolic ways to help children safely project unrecognized feelings.

Michelle loved animals. Horseback riding was her special activity, and her dog, Harley, was one of the loves of her life. We decided to write a story about animals and have each animal talk about its feelings. Then Michelle drew a picture about it. She allowed the animals to speak many of the thoughts and feelings she had kept inside after the death of her mom. The following is Michelle's story.

*"Mr. Squiggle and His Animals"*

*The dogs are very **jealous** of Mr. Squiggle and his other animals because he pays more attention to them. "Look at him, he pays more attention to his horse and cow than us," they said.*

*The cat **loves** Mr. Squiggle because she gets to do things.*

` *The fish gets very* **scared** *because where he lives there's a lot of thunderstorms. He's afraid of the noise.*

*The hermit crab is* **shocked** *because he thinks Mr. Squiggle pays too much attention to the other animals.*

*The cow is* **ashamed***. He did something so bad he's grounded for a month.*

*The bunny is* **sad***. She thinks that Mr. Squiggle loves the other animals more than her.*

*The chickens are* **happy** *because they are taken care of. The horse feels like that too.*

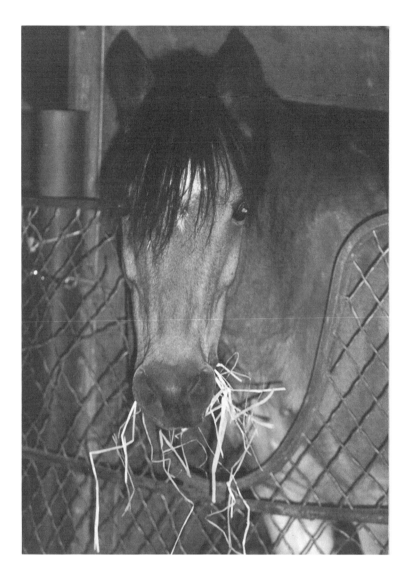

Michelle's dog, hermit crab, and bunny felt shocked, jealous, and sad that Mr. Squiggle might love some of the other animals more than them. I asked Michelle if she felt that anyone in her life did that to her. "Well, my dad pays more attention to my brother then he does to me. I think he likes him better than me," she replied. "How does that make you feel?" I asked. "Jealous and sad,"she replied. We invited Dad in and shared these feelings.

Michelle also enjoyed using her imagination through storytelling. One day she was waving the magic wand I have in my office and wishing she could create a magical place on earth. The following is her story about such a special place.

*"The Most Magical Place on Earth"*

*Once there was a girl named Michelle. She came to a magical place where everything came true. She wanted a rainbow beside her every day. She wanted a house made with sticks and a sun with sunglasses. The rainbow would have a cloud and a pot of gold. The house was small on the outside and big on the inside. She hoped one day to live in a mansion bigger than any kingdom you've ever seen. She would live with her flowers. There are lots of animals.*

*Michelle*

*P.S. If I lived in a magical place I'd make nice people never die and bring a few people back from the dead. I'd like to meet God.*

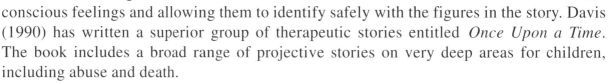

She began to explain that this place was where she pictured her mom being. It was safe and beautiful, and Michelle can revisit in her mind whenever she chooses.

**Ways to Help Children with Therapeutic Stories**

1. *Use therapeutic stories.* These stories are a powerful method of reaching children's unconscious feelings and allowing them to identify safely with the figures in the story. Davis (1990) has written a superior group of therapeutic stories entitled *Once Upon a Time*. The book includes a broad range of projective stories on very deep areas for children, including abuse and death.

2. *Tell a story box.* In a decorative box, place objects such as the following:

*people*—man, woman, children,
*weapons*—hammer, gun, ax,
*animals*—dog, cat, pig, wolf, and
*power figures*—superman, monsters, dinosaurs.

Children can pick one or several objects and create a story. The therapist and the child can alternate in creating a continuous story.

3. *Make up a therapeutic story.* Therapeutic stories speak to children in a metaphorical way that is very powerful. Stories open the door to the unconscious by allowing the child to relate to the story without calling attention to himself or herself.

We can create a story that speaks to the child about his or her particular issue without using the exact facts. If a 6-year-old boy was verbally abused by his dad, who later committed suicide, we can create a story about a 9-year-old boy whose dad embarrassed him by screaming at him at baseball practice. His dad got arrested for robbery and put in prison. "How do you think this boy felt about his dad not being at home anymore?"

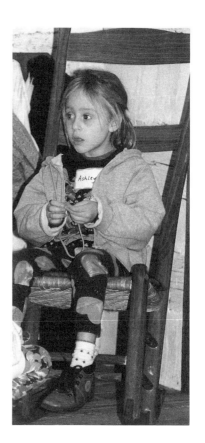

## VISUALIZATION TECHNIQUES

*Visualizion techniques* allow children to use their imagination to re-create healthy thoughts and reduce anxiety.

Visualization techniques can be an effective method of working with grief. Children can visualize painful or disturbing feelings and then, through guiding their imagery, begin to substitute more positive visual memories and find inner resources for strength. We can combine imagination, fairy tales, and metaphor to create a powerful tool for change. Children can use their natural gift of imagination to reduce anxiety and establish helpful thoughts.

---

**When leading the child through the visualization, it is important to**

- *acknowledge* feelings and thoughts,
- *emphasize* positive affirmations,
- *incorporate* all of the five senses, and
- *remind* the child that this is a safe place to which he or she can return whenever he or she wants.

---

Visualization or guided imagery can empower the child to create his or her own internal ways of dealing with fears, scary obstacles, distances, and absences. Children can experience this peaceful, magical place within their minds and realize they have the internal power to re-create it again and again.

**Procedure**

In order to facilitate visualization, make the following suggestions to the child.

*"Close your eyes."* (Be sure the child is comfortable with closing the eyes; some children do not like to do that.)

*"Begin a 'tummy breath' by starting all the way down in the tummy and blowing out a big breath. Do this three or four times."* (These yoga-like breathing exercises can be helpful in promoting a relaxed state for some children.)

*"We are going to go on a little trip in our imagination. We can stop any time you want to. Just tell me. For now let's relax and enjoy ourselves."*

*"Imagine a place you would love in a natural setting. Try to see it in your mind. What does it look like? Look around you. What do you see? Where are you? Who is with you? What colors do you see? What is the weather? How does it smell? Feel the sand or soil. Does it feel smooth against your fingers? Does the wind blow against your face? Is it sunny? Feel the breeze on your face. Can you hear the birds? What are they saying?"*

Try to incorporate all of the five senses when leading the child through the visualization.

*"Open your eyes and draw a picture about the place you have imagined."* (Remind children that this is a safe place in their mind to which they can return whenever they want to do so.)

**Joshua's Visualization**

Joshua is a 6-year-old boy who has talked about some scary thoughts associated with his mom's cancer. Josh says, "When I'm away from my mom and don't know how she is, I get scared that she might get sick and go back to the hospital." When he was asked to tell about his scary feelings, he described them as big old dirty black spots. The following is a summary of a visualization or "closed eye story" his mom created to help him transform his fears into a safe place. This technique can be adopted for children who have experienced a significant death, abandonment, or serious illness of a loved one.

This visualization was effective in empowering Joshua to use his rich imagination to deal with his fears and anxieties. It is a technique that can be used well with such mentally sensitive children.

---

The story (adapted from *The Search for the King*) takes place in a magical land with beautiful birds and a colored forest. There is a river separating the child from the loved one and a monster that guards it, not letting anyone across. *The river is the barrier* to the loved one and *the monster represents the child's fears and scary thoughts*. A magical white eagle comes to help the child cross over the river to be with Mom. *The eagle symbolizes inner strength* that can rise above fears. Together they create a giant rainbow of love and warmth that climbs over the river. *The rainbow is faith in one's self.*

This place of safety lives within the heart of the child. The beautiful eagle can be called upon at any time to again visit the magical land.

---

This story can be modified into a shorter version or used for several sessions as a continuous activity. A tape recording of the visualization can be made and given to the child to keep and use whenever he or she would like.

This visualization also can be projected onto clay or sand table figures. Children can retell the story with emphasis on the affirmations of transcending fear through positive imagery within themselves.

Children can draw the magical land and the magical way it looks. "Draw how you felt before you crossed the river and after you crossed the river."

Children also can make paper bag puppets of the characters. They can act out the story or role-play different parts.

## SILENCE

*Silence* can be used to help children affirm their feelings.

Jennifer was an 11-year-old client whose dad had died of a sudden heart attack. She burst into my office during the first week of school, enraged at her new teacher. She had bravely decided to tell this new teacher that her dad had just died. Her teacher never responded to her. She began punching the punching bag in the office and crying at the same time. "How could she not answer me?" she questioned. "Fear," I thought to myself. Later, when Jennifer had expressed and acted out some of her feelings, we discussed the idea that people's fears of not knowing what to say or of feeling bad themselves can create their silence. "What do you wish the teacher would have done?" I asked. "Given me a hug and said 'I'm sorry.' "

An incident with a 15-year-old client whose dad also had died suddenly in a car crash surfaced about the same time. Debbie was deeply saddened by her father's sudden death. She had had an extremely close relationship with him, sharing life together intellectually, emotionally, and socially. Memories were painful. I usually invite kids to bring in pictures of their loved one, and we can share memories together. Debbie said that she did not want to do so the first time I asked her. The next session I again mentioned that she might bring in a picture of her dad.

She declined, stating she did not want to and when she was ready, she would let me know. We worked together many months. I remained silent about the picture, respecting Debbie's wisdom of knowing her own timing in her grief process.

Finally, we had decided it was time for Debbie to leave grief therapy. At our final meeting, I usually give the children a little good-bye gift. Debbie's was a picture frame. As she opened her gift, she handed me a wonderful picture of her dad that just happened to fit into the frame. Debbie taught me a great lesson—trust the inner wisdom of the grieving child.

 Jennifer's and Debbie's stories illustrate the power of *silence*. Silence given out of fear creates hurt, rage, and deep sadness. Silence given out of respect and love creates trust and inner strength. We, as caregivers, cannot fix the circumstances with which these children are faced. We can acknowledge and support them in their grief.

## MEMORY WORK

Use *memory work* with symbolic figures, drawings, and storytelling as a projective tool to release frozen feelings.

Jimmy, age 8, was a child whose father had been murdered. Before his death, Jimmy's dad moved out of the home but remained a strong disciplinarian. Jimmy's memories of his dad's frequent anger remained buried deep inside Jimmy.

Jimmy had great difficulty verbalizing his feelings. The use of projective tools became an important ingredient in our work together. The following is a picture Jimmy drew in a memory book showing life before his dad's death. Jimmy never drew real people, only cartoon characters. The picture shows Dad telling Jimmy, "Go to bed," and Jimmy saying, "Help."

During one session, Jimmy began making a story using symbolic figures (army men and power figures). In the story, the helplessness in the previous picture changed to powerfulness as he was encouraged to act out his fantasy with the objects. The following is the story he told:

> *"Once upon a time there was a dragon named Gonzilla. He was mean, hairy, and breathed fire. The people in the town were scared. They hired Jimmy, The Powerful, to protect them."*

We took a photograph of Jimmy's figures and left it with his display for others to see. He asked many times what other kids had said about his story and was glad to hear they used his idea to make stories of their own.

Sometimes Jimmy would not or could not communicate. He would not speak at all or used only one-word responses. One day we decided to make a scribble drawing. Jimmy began scribbling on a piece of paper furiously. When he finished, I asked him to think of a title for his work. "A Tornado" was his reply. "If the tornado could talk, what would it say?" I asked. "Help me," he sighed. The following is his drawing.

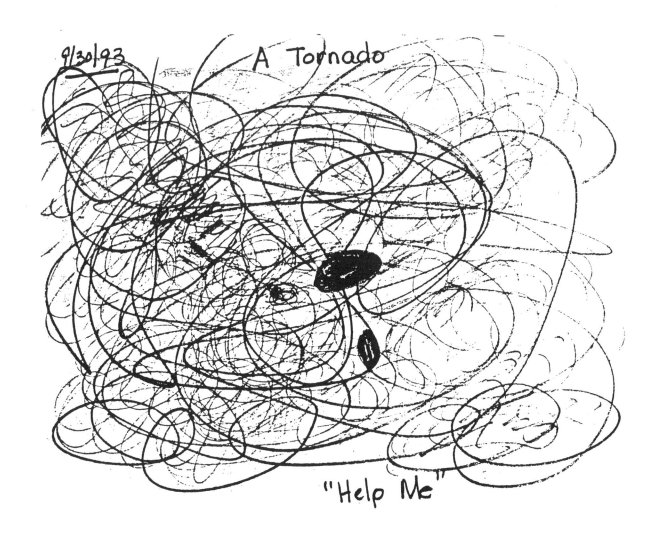

One day Jimmy came in filled with anger he could barely control. He began punching the punching bag with nothing to say. Any attempt I made to engage in verbal communication was met with no response. I began to tell him a make believe story about a child I knew who was very angry at his dad.

> *"The Dad had left home to go to the war in Viet Nam. He used to punish his son a lot and make him clean his room. Now every time the boy walked by his dad's picture, can you guess what he would say?"*

Jimmy burst into a blast of words in a way I had never heard him do before or since. This was his response to the question.

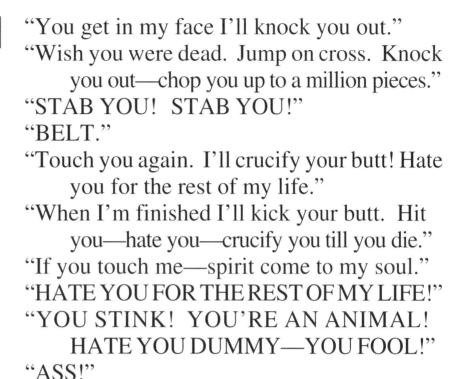

"You get in my face I'll knock you out."

"Wish you were dead.  Jump on cross.  Knock you out—chop you up to a million pieces."

"STAB YOU!  STAB YOU!"

"BELT."

"Touch you again.  I'll crucify your butt!  Hate you for the rest of my life."

"When I'm finished I'll kick your butt.  Hit you—hate you—crucify you till you die."

"If you touch me—spirit come to my soul."

"HATE YOU FOR THE REST OF MY LIFE!"

"YOU STINK!  YOU'RE AN ANIMAL!  HATE YOU DUMMY—YOU FOOL!"

"ASS!"

The rage and violent thoughts that spewed out of Jimmy's lips filled the room.  When he finished his forceful response, he became silent again.

---

Jimmy is one of millions of children on the planet whose *complicated grief* is getting in the way of his functioning as a normal child.  By using the projective techniques of drawing, storytelling, and symbolic figures that allow him to begin to uncover the *shame and terror* he holds associated with his dad and his brutal death, Jimmy can begin the long journey of separating these circumstances from the actual death of his dad.  Jimmy's *hidden rage* emerged behind his silence, bringing feelings into the open to be seen and witnessed.  The first drop to the *meltdown process* had begun.

---

**Tools for Memory Work with Children**

1.  Use *memory books*.  Memory books are participatory workbooks that enable children to draw and write their feelings and thoughts in an interactive way.  They can be purchased commercially or made to meet the specific needs of the child.  The following is a story that accompanies a page from a memory book.  The story and picture tell of how Danny's dad died and the way Danny remembers that he was told about the death.

*My dad, Michael, got killed. There was an accident. His car hit a tree. He's dead. He is in heaven.*

*My mom told me on December 1st. When my mom told me I felt sad, but I didn't cry. I was shocked. The police had come and told my mother.*

*I said, "Why? What happened?" "He died," Mom said. "He died because there was ice. He slid into a tree."*

*Danny*

*P.S. I like to wear my Dad's shirt. It makes me feel good.*

---

### Commercial memory books for young children:

- *Memory Book for Bereaved Children* (Braza, 1988)
- *A Child Remembers* (Traisman, 1994)
- *When Someone Very Special Dies* (Heegaard, 1988)

### Commercial memory books for teenagers:

- *Fire in My Heart, Ice in My Veins* (Traisman, 1992)
- *Facing Change* (O'Toole, 1995)

---

2. Use *memory boxes* or *a memory table*. We can help children create memory boxes or a memory table to provide places to store or share treasured items of their loved ones. Memory boxes can be made from a shoe box that is painted and decorated to house precious belongings. A memory table can be displayed in a child's room or special part of the house with pictures and things that are meaningful to them.

3. Use *photos*, *videos*, and *tape recordings*. Photographs, videos, and tape recordings are concrete ways to stimulate visual and auditory memories of a loved one. Making a photo album of pictures children choose and titling it "My Life" brings in a clear picture of times and events shared as well as a motivation for discussion. Videos and tape recordings of a loved one are very precious. So often kids feel they might forget how their person looked and sounded. These are wonderful ways to help remember.

4. Have children make a list of the facts or *unanswered questions* they want to know about the death of a person who has been important in their lives. Help them *develop the resources* to find the answers through parents, relatives, counselors, books, etc.

5. Let children *tell how they were told* about an illness or death. Make a chart that explains when they felt *included or left out*. Have children draw or write about ways they *wish* they had been told about or included in the illness or death of their loved one.

6. *Linking objects* are important memory tools for children. A loved one's key chain, sweater, drawing, and diary are concrete symbolic forms to help kids feel closer to the person who has died by providing tangible representations to hold and cherish.

Eleven-year-old Nancy felt her mom was with her every time she saw a butterfly. Her dad gave her a linking object, a necklace of a butterfly, for her to wear every day to help her feel Mom's presence.

Sammy was a 6-year-old who became enraged when his mom said she was selling the car his grandfather gave them before he died. Grandpa had said the car would always protect him and keep him safe. Selling the car triggered feelings of Grandpa's death. Sam and Mom discussed several linking objects such as a windshield wiper or an armrest to help remember Grandpa. They eventually agreed upon Sam's taking photos of the car, creating an ongoing reminder of his grandfather's love.

## SUMMARY OF WAYS TO HELP CHILDREN

1.  Use *visualization techniques* to allow children to create positive images.

2.  Use *concrete objects* to symbolically express feelings of nurturing and love that have suddenly been cut off.

3.  Use *reality checks* such as medical checkups and phone calls to the home to provide sustained reassurance to someone in a very fragile state.

4.  Use and respect the *belief system* of the child as a support and framework to assimilate and hold the experience of life and death.

5.  Create *normalcy* whenever possible by emphasizing that overwhelming fears of death and worries of abandonment are absolutely okay and are a reasonable reaction in coping with the unreasonable.

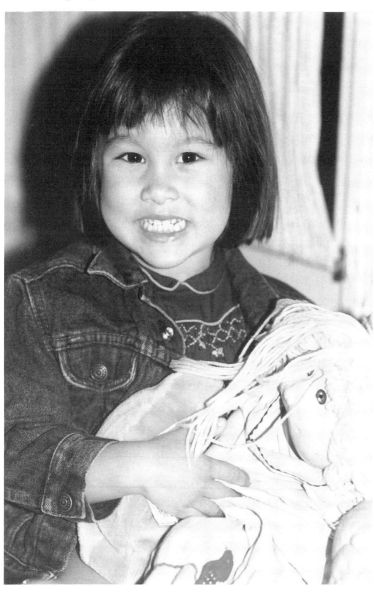

6. Use *role-playing techniques*. Children having experienced a complicated grief usually have great difficulty directly expressing feelings. Often shock, rage, and terror stemming from how the person died block the flow of feelings. Plays, puppetry, clay figures, sand table stories, and dollhouses with figures and furniture are valuable tools that allow kids to project unresolved feelings in a more open way.

7. Use *dreams*. Dreams are a fertile ground to understand denied powerful emotions that can then be brought out into the open through stories and drawings.

8. Use *memory work*. Using photographs, newspaper articles, or treasured objects and belongings associated with loved ones who died

will help solidify feelings and bring these feelings to the surface. Making memory books and memory boxes will help initiate discussions with children and provide a concrete form for valuable memories.

9. Use *projective tools* such as play figures, drawings, and storytelling to help release frozen feelings.

10.  Use *silence*.  Silence is a powerful tool for allowing a child to own his or her feelings rather than be told how he or she should think and feel.

11. Create *rituals*.  Children can create symbolic ways of sending love to a person who has died.  Sending a balloon with an attached note, floating a note in a bottle in the ocean, ringing a special bell at a special time, eating at that person's favorite restaurant, or singing his or her favorite song can help create an inner bond of love that lives through time.

**Chapter 7**

# SAYING GOOD-BYE: WAYS TO INCLUDE CHILDREN IN A FUNERAL OR MEMORIAL

- Play area for children ■ Bubbles to send off ■ Memory bags
- Children's music ■ Freedom to leave/freedom to participate
- Table for drawings and stories
- Comfortable seating with friends and family

## OPENING A MEMORIAL SERVICE TO CHILDREN

Breaking the silence on funerals and memorial services by *including children* is an idea whose time has come. So many times I have received calls from parents asking if children should come to a funeral or memorial service. I feel that not only should they come, but that the memorial service and funeral can become shared family experiences.

---

### ANDREW'S DEATH

Andrew was a child who died suddenly of a rare virus on a family vacation in the Boston area. Friends and family were not prepared for this shocking and unexpected death. Andrew was 6 years old and had just completed kindergarten. The *shock* of his death needed to be recognized and processed before the overwhelming feeling of loss for Andrew could be honored. The memorial service was a vehicle for expression of this complicated grief.

## PREPARING THE COMMUNITY

Andrew's parents carefully and consciously wrote the following letter (reprinted here with permission). It was sent to the parents of every child at Andrew's school before Andrew's parents returned home from Boston. Their letter tells of the facts of Andrew's death and the events surrounding his illness.

*Dear Friends,*

*Many of you have asked "What happened to Andrew?" We would like to share with you the last few weeks. We were vacationing. Andrew was happy and healthy, riding his boogey board on the ocean waves, fishing, and playing in the great out-of-doors. He had a slight fever for about a day and a half so we gave him Tylenol.*

*When Andrew went to bed Wednesday evening, August 10, he was energetic and feeling fine. During the night he complained of shoulder cramps, a stiff neck, and aching legs. Early in the morning, we took him to the hospital. He was tentatively diagnosed with spinal meningitis and medically evacuated by helicopter to another hospital in Boston. His father Doug rode with him.*

*The next days were a roller coaster ride; Andrew's condition quickly worsened and then appeared to stabilize. We hoped that, in time, the virus would pass through the body. We were with Andrew the entire time, talking, singing, caressing, reading to him. He was in no pain and knew that we were there. Andrew received excellent medical care, from loving physicians, nurses, and medical technicians. On the afternoon of Tuesday, August 16, Andrew passed away. His brain and his heart had been irreversibly damaged by an undetermined virus which caused meningoencephalomyelitis and myocarditis.*

*We know for sure that Andrew's illness was not contagious; no other family members or friends have been sick. Nor did Andrew have any predisposing medical conditions that contributed to his illness. It is possible that further medical tests will give us more information about the precise virus.*

*On August 20, we had a lovely funeral service for Andrew at a monastery chapel in Cambridge, Massachusetts. A small group of Andrew's family and friends joined us. On August 22, Andrew's ashes were interred at the cemetery, next to his paternal grandfather. Andrew had always loved the story of King Tut's mummy; we, too, buried many gifts with Andrew, including favorite books, music tapes, family photos, toys, and shells, rocks, and sand from the beach. Later, in September or October, we will have a memorial service in the Washington, DC, area. Friends of Andrew—of all ages—will be invited to celebrate Andrew's life and share their memories in drawings, poems, songs, and other joyful ways.*

*We grieve for our beautiful son; but we feel blessed that we had six wonderful years with him. A memorial fund will be established at Andrew's school to provide additional playground facilities. Also, a memorial fund will be established at a special hospital to establish an early childhood library in the pediatrics unit.*

*We are so grateful for your continued love and support.*

*Love,*
*Judy and Doug*

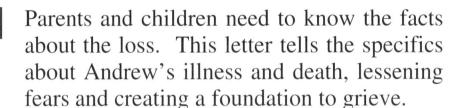

Parents and children need to know the facts about the loss. This letter tells the specifics about Andrew's illness and death, lessening fears and creating a foundation to grieve.

## PREPARING THE SCHOOL

Andrew's school included his parents' letter with this letter (reprinted here with permission) from the headmaster to all members of the school community. Additional written information and resources on children and grief also were provided.

*August 25, 1994*

*Dear Green Acres Parents:*

*Yesterday, I received this fax from Judy and Doug, parents of Andrew, who was a student in our kindergarten last year. Andrew passed away on August 16 after a brief illness. Because Judy and Doug have written such a lovely and moving letter, I would like their own words to tell you the story of what happened to Andrew.*

*I know that there will be many questions about how to talk to your children about Andrew's death. Many younger children may be fearful, and many parents may be uncomfortable addressing death with their children. I have talked with Linda Goldman, one of our parents and the co-director of The Center for Loss and Grief Therapy. She has passed along to me the attachments that offer some advice for talking about death with children. You might want to read her book:* Life and Loss: A Guide to Help Grieving Children. *On the first day of school, a clinical social worker will be available to talk to children who are anxious or fearful or simply want to talk. A physician will be willing to answer medical questions for parents who may have them.*

*Our community mourns the loss of Andrew. He was a vital, intelligent young fellow who loved the playground. Personally, I will miss him. He and I connected on a special level. I will not forget the afternoon of the Olympics when he and I watched the older children on the "Slip and Slide."*

*Judy and Doug will be back in the Washington area soon. I know that they will appreciate your caring and supportive wishes.*

*Sincerely,*
*Arnold S. C., Headmaster*

## PREPARING THE PARENTS

A meeting was held at Andrew's school for all interested parents and faculty. Information and appropriate resources were presented on how young children grieve. Feelings were shared about Andrew's death as it affected the children, and adults expressed their own feelings, fears, and vulnerabilities. The parents were given the following suggestions on how to prepare the children for the memorial service.

1. *Tell the children the facts* about Andrew's death.
2. *Share your feelings* of grief with your child.
3. *Allow children to express feelings* and commemorate through drawings and stories.
4. *Describe what will happen* at the memorial service.
5. *Invite the child* to join you in coming to the service, but never force.

6. *Explain that the children can participate* if they feel like it by telling a story about Andrew or something special they remember. They can share artwork or poetry. They do not have to participate if they do not feel like it.

7. *Remind them that they can participate* in children's songs and art activities, and that people they know will be there.

8. *If they feel uncomfortable, they can leave* (and those adults who accompany the child to the service should be prepared to leave if the child wants to do so).

9. Some people may be sad and cry, and you [the child] may be sad and cry. That's okay. *However, you may not feel sad and may not cry.* That's okay too.

10. *Read children's resources* such as *Life and Loss: A Guide to Help Grieving Children* (Goldman, 1994) and *About Dying* (Stein, 1974) to help prepare children and answer questions.

11. As much as possible, *share what will happen ahead of time.*

12. *Encourage* the children to ask *questions.*

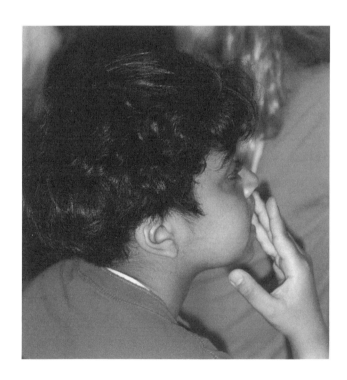

## PREPARING THE MEMORIAL SERVICE

Andrew's parents then began preparing a very child-oriented memorial service to celebrate Andrew's life as well as commemorate his death. They told parents what the ceremony would be like, so that the parents, in turn, could tell their children what to expect. A notice also was put in the school newspaper.

While Andrew's parents went through all of the normal pain and anguish and stages of deep personal grief, this remarkable couple summoned their deep love for their son, Andrew, to create a loving tribute to his life. In so doing, their own grief process was enriched as were the grief processes of all others who were involved with the memorial service.

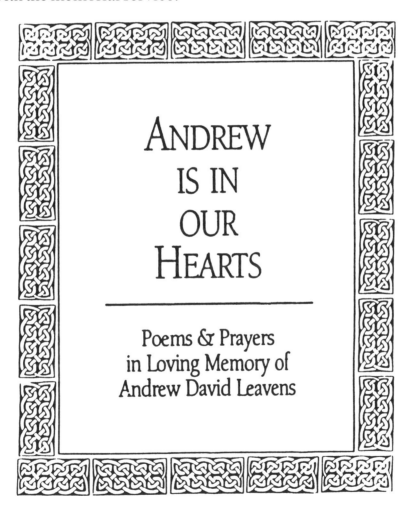

ANDREW
IS IN
OUR
HEARTS

Poems & Prayers
in Loving Memory of
Andrew David Leavens

## PREPARING THE CHILDREN

Andrew's memorial service served as a model for me of what is possible when parents choose to commemorate and honor the dignity of their child's life with a true respect for all children. *It was a celebration of Andrew's life as well as a commemoration of his death.*

While there certainly was sadness, the service held a warmth and invited openness that allowed children of all ages, adult friends, family members, coworkers of Andrew's parents, school representatives, and Andrew's parents themselves to freely and spontaneously participate. Stories were told, songs were sung, and poetry was read that acknowledged the wonderful life that was Andrew's.

Children and adults sat on the floor. Chairs also were set up in the back of the room. Families were together. Children could lie down, stand up, or leave if they chose to do so. They did not have to participate. They could if they wanted to. They could go outside and blow bubbles or play. The children made their own choices as long as the service was respected. A parent or caring adult was prepared to leave with each designated child. Children's artwork and stories were displayed on tables and walls. They told of memories and love and sorrow for the children's friend Andrew.

We have selected these poems and prayers to capture the love and appreciation we have for Andrew. We celebrate his energy and curiosity, his joy in physical movement, his friendship, his ability to share and to help others share, his humor and love of nonsense, his understanding of good and evil and his trust in the potential for good, his respect for nature, his balance and grace, his daring, and his sense of the spiritual.

To see the world through the eyes of a child is truly a gift that opens our hearts.

Love,

*Judy and Doug*

## SHARING MEMORIES

Andrew's parents made a booklet of favorite poems and prayers for each family to take home. The following are a few of the many loving remembrances shared.

The following was shared by Jillian, Andrew's sister:

*Some people come into our lives and quickly go,*
*Some stay for awhile, leave footprints on our hearts,*
*and we are never, ever the same.*

Flavia Weedn

## Andrew is in my heart.

(written by Chris, age 7, Andrew's good friend)

Chris' mom was crying one night and Chris wanted to know why. "I'm crying because I'm sad that I will never be able to see Andrew," she said. "Don't worry," he replied. "I can see Andrew whenever I want, because he's always in my heart."

## POEM [2]

I loved my friend
He went away from me
There's nothing more to say.
The poem ends,
Soft as it began—
I loved my friend.

Langston Hughes

## THE MEMORIAL SERVICE

Children and teenagers shared their thoughts, feelings, pictures, and stories. Their ages ranged from 5 to 16.

Some children shared their photo collection about special times with Andrew.

Some children cried. Some children did not want to participate. Some children felt they wanted to leave. That was okay too.

Some children and teenagers opened up their hearts and read poems they had written.

Some children and teenagers could not share. They were given a voice from a caring adult, such as Andrew's dad, who read their letters.

Andrew's adult friends and family shared their remembrances of Andrew's life.

Andrew's class shared their gift—each child's handprint on a quilt for Andrew's parents.

Community support was very meaningful. Andrew's school principal spoke of his memories of Andrew.

Andrew's parents shared their love for and experiences with Andrew. They told funny stories about their son.

Andrew's teachers and friends sang many of Andrew's favorite songs. They invited the

children and their families to join in if they felt comfortable. Songs included "The Earth Is Mine," "When the Rain Comes Down," "I'm Being Eaten by a Boa Constrictor," and "The Garden Song." At the very end of the memorial service, people held hands and sang "Friends, Friends."

## AFTER THE SERVICE

After the service, the children were guided in making several hands-on commemorations of Andrew if they wanted. There was a crafts table where the children could draw pictures, write letters, or share stories about Andrew. Bubbles were provided for the children. They could take them outside to blow in remembrance of Andrew.

"Memory bags" were made for each child who attended. The bags were filled with treats (like pieces of candy) that Andrew's parents felt he would have liked to give his friends.

The room was filled with photos of Andrew, Andrew's own artwork, and the artwork and stories of Andrew's friends. The children could walk through the room freely and experience Andrew's life visually.

Favorite toys and books of Andrew's were on display, as well as many photos of him, his family, and his friends. Shown on page 132 is a picture that Andrew made at age 4 ½.

Each family also took home the booklet of poems and prayers prepared by Andrew's parents. Many families read selections as a way to remember Andrew. Classmates and friends read these poems at school or quiet times at home. One friend was inspired to create the remembrance shown here.

The children who attended Andrew's memorial service appeared to gain a great gift—the gift of inner strength. Knowing they could participate and be very present with adults in a community remembrance of their friend gave them the awareness of how to honor Andrew's life. *Knowing how to honor Andrew's life gives these children a way to value and respect their own lives.* This undoubtedly will help them know and be prepared for other life and death experiences they will face.

## COMMEMORATING AFTER THE MEMORIAL SERVICE OR FUNERAL

Commemorating is one of the four psychological tasks of grieving (Goldman, 1994). We can help children accomplish this important task by enabling them to actively participate in the memorial service or funeral. We also can present rituals and other tangible ways to continue the commemoration process. The importance and effectiveness of *offering children an ongoing concrete way to remember* a loved one who has died cannot be emphasized enough.

In the case of Andrew, his parents and school decided to continue remembering his life through the process of creating a new playground in his memory. The site would be the very place where Andrew played the most. The project was designed to involve the community, family, and school children and personnel.

The school children would be asked for ideas and designs on how they would like the new playground to be. The parents would be asked to offer expertise and skills in the creation and production of the project. Families would be invited to come together in building the equipment. Teachers and school personnel were encouraged to join. Truly Andrew will continue to be acknowledged and honored as children work on the playground, watch the new addition to the school being built, and play on this new source of fun for years to come. Many of the children will remember their experience of helping friends and family create a living tribute to Andrew.

## A Playground in Memory of Andrew

The following is an excerpt from Andrew's school newsletter. It describes the plan for a memorial playground for Andrew.

*Plans are underway to build a playground structure in memory of Andrew. Manufacturers of playground equipment have been consulted, plus suggestions have been solicited from faculty and K-Gr.4 students. Frequently and enthusiastically mentioned ideas from children were mazes, monkey swings, forts, castles, haunted houses, climbing ropes, and ziplines. Some children even drew pictures of what they'd like to have on the playground.*

*Over the past few months, Andrew's parents have been meeting with the administration and development staff to find easy ways to translate these wonderful, imaginative ideas into reality. This week a working model of a playground maze was shown to the classes. The children were excited and suggested adding mirrors, banners, and tunnels. Over the summer, plans will be further developed. We hope that one weekend next fall, families can join together to help construct the new playground structure.*

This memorial playground was completed in December 1995. Parents, children, faculty, and friends came together in sunshine and snow to complete this wonderful tribute to Andrew.

This school-based memorial playground created a living sense of community and extended family by including the following in its planning and creation:

- children's ideas and input,
- school faculty and staff,
- parents' skills and abilities, and
- community activities.

# REMEMBERING SPECIAL DAYS

*Rituals are very powerful* and are especially important when remembering loved ones on special days. Children's play incorporates the use of rituals as a physical way of *providing a structure* for the energy they wish to create. We can provide the opportunity for the children to continue to *use concrete forms* that hold the space that allows continued remembrance and honoring of the people they have loved.

### Andrew's Birthday Remembrance

Andrew's parents carefully prepared for the first birthday after his death. Much time, energy, remembering, and love went into the creation of this special day. His parents decided to include children in their commemoration and *encouraged expression* of children's ideas about how to celebrate Andrew's birthday.

Several of Andrew's special friends had been talking about his upcoming birthday. Andrew's cousin Cristina reminisced about last year's birthday and remembered many of Andrew's favorite things.

She wished she could invent a machine that had a button she could press and bring Andrew back to life. Cristina wanted to make a cake with his favorite rainbow sprinkles decorated on top. A neighborhood playmate wanted to get balloons. She said, "They must be green—Andrew's favorite color!"

So Andrew's parents followed the lead of these children and, all together, they planned a birthday party. The children were invited to make a birthday cake for Andrew with his mom. Each friend participated in creating the cake and decorating in ways Andrew would have liked. Pictures were displayed from many of Andrew's earlier birthday parties. They remembered one of Andrew's favorite hiding games and decided to play it.

Goody bags were provided, and balloons were launched by the children to symbolically send their love through time. The children made a circle around the balloons and began chanting spontaneously, "We love Andrew, we love Andrew" as they sent the balloons into the air. They then were allowed to choose plants to place in their own back yards as an ongoing remembrance that they could see and watch grow.

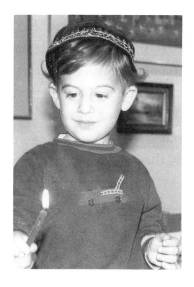

## WAYS CHILDREN CAN COMMEMORATE

- Plant a flower or tree.
- Blow bubbles.
- Send up a balloon.
- Light a candle.
- Say a prayer.
- Write a poem, story, or song about the loved one who died. Send it to the loved one's family.
- Talk into a tape recorder or make a video of memories.
- Make cookies or cake and take them to the family of the person who has died.
- Create a mural or collage about the life of the person who has died.

## SUMMARY OF WHAT A CHILD-ORIENTED MEMORIAL SERVICE OR FUNERAL SHOULD INCLUDE

### Preparing the Children

1. Give the child the facts about the death.

2. Invite the child to be included in the event.

3. Give the child the choice of participation in the service by sharing memories.

4. Allow the child to be a part of decision making. What pictures or favorite memories would he or she like displayed?

5. Prepare the child for the service.

Describe how it will look.
Describe what people will do.
Allow children to ask questions.

6. Read resources such as *Thank You for Coming to Say Good-bye* (Roberts & Johnson, 1994). This book contains good ideas to help adults include children. Read *Tell Me, Papa* (Johnson & Johnson, 1990) to children as a means to inform them about funerals.

7. Remind children that they can leave if they feel uncomfortable. Set up a plan ahead of time.

8. Emphasize that some people feel sad, some may not. Either way is okay.

## Preparing the Service

1. Fill the room with memory tables that have the loved one's pictures and treasured items.

2. Display commemorative letters and drawings that others have made for and about the loved one.

3. Create a booklet of feelings about the person who died that can include children's work as well as adults'.

4. Arrange to include songs appropriate for children to sing in the ceremony.

5. Display a seating arrangement whereby people can sit on chairs and also sit on the floor together as families.

6. Include spaces in the service in which children can participate in sharing stories and drawings if they choose.

7. Provide an art table that children can go to after the service to draw or write letters.

8. Create memory bags to give to the children.

9. Provide bubbles and/or balloons for children to send off symbolically for their loved one.

10. Bring flowers as a way of remembering the continuing cycle of life.

## RESOURCES TO HELP CHILDREN WITH FUNERALS AND MEMORIALS

*Pablo Remembers,* by George Ancona (1993), is a wonderful explanation of the Mexican custom of celebrating of El Dia de Los Muertos, The Day of the Dead, by celebrating the life of a loved one over and over again.

*Tell Me, Papa*, by Joy and Marv Johnson (1990), talks in very simple and clear language about death, funerals, and how children feel about both.

*A Candle for Grandpa: A Guide to the Jewish Funeral for Children and Parents,* by David Techner and Judith Hirt-Manheimer (1993), helps comfort children after the death of a loved one. The story tells of a Jewish funeral and burial practice in clear and meaningful ways.

*You Hold Me and I'll Hold You*, by Jo Carson (1992), is a simple story for young children about a young girl's feelings of wanting to hold and be held at a memorial service.

*Thank You for Coming to Say Good-bye*, by Janice Roberts and Joy Johnson (1994), is an excellent source of information to help caring adults involve children in funeral services.

# Chapter 8

## EDUCATORS CAN HELP: LET'S GET INVOLVED

■    Resources and support for the bereaved student    ■  Crisis intervention—
coping with a student death   ■    Procedures for coping with homicide and other
violent deaths  ■  Suicide prevention, intervention, and postvention  ■   Teaching
children to prevent abuse  ■  In-service staff training on children and loss
■  School memorial commemorations  ■  School-based loss and grief curricula

# RESOURCES AND SUPPORT FOR THE BEREAVED STUDENT

Margaret's dad died in a car accident. He was declared by the police to be a drunk driver, speeding at 60 mph in a 25-mph zone. A year later, Margaret was diagnosed as having ADD (Attention Deficit Disorder) and told that she must repeat fourth grade. She was an angry and disruptive child, not willing to socialize and not wanting to do schoolwork. Margaret worried about her mom and wanted to be with her a lot. Her mom worried because Margaret had never cried over her dad's death. "Life's just not fair," Margaret would constantly say. "We're not a family without Dad."

**What Can the School Do?**

1. Teachers, counselors, and administrators can *let Margaret know that they care* and are there for her if she needs them. Caring adults need to say words to children without expecting or inviting a response. Reaching out lays the groundwork for future communication. Most importantly, they need to *listen,* and the grieving child needs to feel heard.

2. Educators need to *prepare the class* for the grieving student's return, maintain contact with the family, and provide space for the grieving student and fellow classmates to express feelings and ask questions. Resources such as O'Toole's (1989) *Growing Through Grief: A K-12 Curriculum to Help Young People Through All Kinds of Grief* is extremely helpful for ideas and insights.

Teachers can *encourage classmates to maintain contact with the grieving child* by calling, sending cards, making pictures or letters, baking cookies, or visiting the home. Classmates need to be given the facts and encouraged to express feelings and fears. Reminders to *welcome the grieving child* and say that they are glad to see him or her means a lot to the grieving child. Encourage kids to listen and share and realize that sadness is normal.

3. Caring adults can *provide resources* such as school personnel, books, grief therapists, and community support groups to help facilitate the grieving process. A teacher may offer help to a bereaved student by suggesting that there are many available people in the school and that he or she can arrange time with them if needed. The school librarian has books on loss and grief. The school counselor has time and resources to offer.

4. School policy could *allow Margaret special consideration* if she becomes overwhelmed with thoughts and feelings. She may need reassurance more often than other children that other family members are safe.

Margaret's teacher can express an awareness that it may be difficult for Margaret to maintain her normal school routine and that the teacher will help modify it by

- allowing her to leave the room if needed,
- allowing her to call home if necessary,
- creating a visit to the school nurse and guidance counselor periodically,
- changing some work assignments,
- assigning a class helper,
- creating some private time in the day, and/or
- giving more academic progress reports.

A helpful resource for teachers is *Grief Comes to Class* by Majel Gliko-Bradon (1992).

5. Teachers need to *be aware of important dates* such as Margaret's dad's birth date and date of death. These are very *difficult days* for her and need to be acknowledged. Holidays such as Father's Day, Christmas, and Valentine's Day may create anxiety, anger, or sadness as they place her loss in the forefront. Invite Margaret to make a symbolic card, light a candle, or create a poem for her dad and join with other children in sharing memories.

6. School personnel need to *be aware and accepting that children's grades usually drop* after the loss of a loved one. This may be the time when impulsivity, distractibility, and hyperactivity emerge. Usually behavioral observations at home and school are the primary criteria for diagnosis of ADD. The following normal grief responses sometimes are mistaken for signals of ADD:

- restlessness in staying seated,
- calling out of turn,
- inability to wait to be responded to,
- incompletion of schoolwork,
- difficulty in following directions,
- poor concentration around external stimuli,
- problems listening and staying on task,
- disorganization,
- reckless physical actions, and
- being overly talkative.

Without the awareness that grief in itself creates inattentiveness and an inability to sit still and concentrate, children can be misdiagnosed with some sort of learning disability. They then can begin the journey of labels and difficulties that place them in a problem zone of being viewed as unable or unwilling to learn. Rather, educators must maintain the necessary patience and respect needed for the grief process of children.

 We, as caring adults, need to be educated in learning the signs of normal and complicated grief. Gaining a respect for and acceptance of the feelings of anxiety or depression that occur with normal grief can be a strong force in differentiating between grief and ADD.

7. *Gathering a comprehensive past history is necessary.*  The loss inventory in my first book, *Life and Loss: A Guide to Help Grieving Children* (Goldman, 1994) is an educational tool that takes a good look at a child's emotional, intellectual, academic, physical, social, and previous family loss history.

*Margaret's dad was a strong disciplinarian.  He often spanked her, leaving marks on her skin, and screamed at her that she was stupid for not understanding her work.  He had a history of alcoholism and financial debt.  His sudden death may have created a complicated grief situation—the shock of her dad's death contrasted with the relief of not being yelled at or hit.  Not crying for over a year was an indicator that something was blocking her from her feelings.*

8. Educators need to *maintain as much consistency and continuity as possible* with the grieving child.  Usually the death of a parent is the catalyst for a chain reaction of multiple

losses. The surviving parent may temporarily not be present due to his or her own grief. Moves, remarriages, or financial changes often occur. The child needs an adult advocate at school available to listen and relate when called upon.

9. The normal grieving process does not stop after a day, a week, a month, or a year. Complicated grief can be present for years and years. Caring adults need to *remember that normal grief and complicated grief symptoms can be present for an entire school year*. The grief process is inhibited when kids are told they need to "move on with their life" or "it's been 6 months; you shouldn't be talking about your loved one so much."

 Any attempt to acknowledge a parent or sibling who died by using his or her name or sharing a memory is a gift we can give the bereaved child.

The following is a story about how a school helped a student commemorate the anniversary of her father's death. A 7-year-old, Molly, was crying as she came into the office at school. It was the anniversary of her dad's death. He had been murdered, and she was feeling sad and wanted to talk to the guidance counselor. Although the counselor was not available, the secretary, Mrs. King, volunteered to help. Molly went on to explain her sadness. "I miss Daddy. I'll never be able to talk to him again," she sobbed.

Mrs. King remembered an idea that had helped her grandchildren when her son had died. She purchased several balloons, including one that said "I Love You." Molly wrote a note to her dad telling about her feelings and attached it to the balloon. Mrs. King took Molly out-

side, and together they sent the balloons off as a symbolic message to Dad. As they looked in the sky before they came in, they were surprised to see a giant rainbow in the sky, ending at the school playground. At the end of the day, Molly returned to the office to thank Mrs. King for her help. "I'm okay now. I think my dad got the message," she said as she skipped down the hall.

10. School teachers, administrators, and other professional personnel need to *establish (create) ways to help students commemorate a death* in the school.

---

## WAYS SCHOOLS CAN COMMEMORATE

■ Create a memory wall with stories and pictures of shared events.
■ Have an assembly about the student.
■ Plant a memory garden.
■ Initiate a scholarship fund.
■ Make a class book of memories and reproduce a copy for the family.
■ Establish an ongoing school fundraiser such as a car wash or bake sale with proceeds going toward the family's designated charity.
■ Place a memorial page and picture in the school yearbook or school newspaper.
■ Send flowers to the grieving family.

---

## WHAT CAN WE DO AS EDUCATORS?

Today's educators face a world where issues of abuse, violence, suicide, homicide, and AIDS must be presented and described to children in an open and clear way by

---

■ helping children understand each topic,
■ creating an awareness that children are not responsible,
■ allowing children the space to grieve their losses caused by complicated grief,
■ teaching children strategies that empower them and maintain their safety, and/or
■ demonstrating nonviolent ways to resolve conflicts, pain, and anger.

---

Children are resilient. Educators need to develop curricula that include definitions of each type of complicated grief. These curricula should include prevention, intervention, and postvention strategies and techniques for school systems. Examples of school-based curricula are listed at the end of this chapter. Resources and pertinent school-, community-, and nationally based supports must be made available for children and parents.

## SUICIDE

Suicide is one type of complicated grief that is all too common among today's youth. The following are signs of at-risk children:

- sudden and pronounced change in behavior;
- threat of suicide or preoccupation with or creation of materials such as artwork or writing indicating that the child does not want to live;
- evidence of substance abuse—drugs, alcohol;
- sudden change of grades;
- avoidance or abandonment of friends;
- angry or tearful outbursts;
- self-destructive behavior;
- inability to sleep or eat;
- over-concern with own health or health of a loved one;
- creation of a will or giving away of important possessions;
- sudden unexplained improvement; and/or
- depression, isolation, or withdrawal.

## SIGNS OF SUICIDAL INTENT

- Active planning of suicide
- Constant preoccupation with death
- Expression of thoughts of worthlessness and desires to end it all
- Giving away possessions
- Talking about one's own funeral
- Sudden unexplained improvement
- Inability to make changes and feelings that there is no way out

## VERBAL SIGNALS

- "Life's not worth living."
- "I'm no good. I don't deserve to live!"
- "I can't see any way out."
- "I wish I were dead."
- "I want to kill myself."
- "What's the use?"

## FRIENDS CAN HELP BY

- Listening
- Asking questions
- Staying calm
- Taking threats seriously
- Telling someone
- Offering suggestions and resources
- Talking about suicide
- Getting help

## Important Concepts for Suicide Discussion

Most of us *think about suicide* at one time in our lives. It is very common. People think these thoughts because they are usually in a lot of emotional pain. People do not need to *act* upon these thoughts.

When a friend says, "I can't take it any more; I wish I could die," what do you feel he or she is really asking for? Kids are crying out for help. They probably want help out of a problem or situation and not necessarily out of life.

Children need to realize that emotional pain has a beginning, a middle, and an end. We can compare bad emotional pain to an awful toothache and how the dentist can help reduce the physical pain. We can help children realize that the intense emotional pain also can subside with help.

We look for reasons for suicide and cannot always find them. We can focus instead on ways to prevent suicide by learning ways to help ourselves and others in emotional pain.

Suicide has different meanings at each developmental stage. We may need to retell, redefine, and explain again at different ages.

## Discussion Questions to Ask After a Suicide

■ If you could see that person one more time, what would you say to him or her? What would you ask?

■ How does this person's death make you feel?

■ What did you lose when your friend died?

■ What is your best memory/your only regret?

■ Have you ever felt that you did not want to live? Do you think that is normal?

■ If you would have known that the person wanted to die, how could you have helped?

## What Can Educators Do During a Suicide Threat?

1. School personnel must *disclose any child's threat* to harm himself or herself or another student and not keep it a secret.

2. School personnel must *report any threat* to a designated school crisis team member or school counselor.

3. School personnel should *contact the at-risk child.* Acknowledge feelings and reinforce decision to share information.

4. The at-risk *child must stay in school* until all information has been processed. A member of the school faculty can *stay with the child* to assure his or her safety.

5. School personnel should *listen* and *encourage talking* from the at-risk child. Use the words *suicide* and *dead.* Ask if the child is thinking about suicide.

6. School personnel must *report threat* to parent or guardian.

7. If parent or guardian does not respond, *protective services can be called.* If it appears to be a medical emergency, report the child to the nurse. If he or she is not there, call *911.*

## VIOLENT DEATH

Violent death may make kids feel the following:

- *anxiety* about being left alone or leaving remaining loved ones,
- *need to relive the violent act* over and over in their minds,
- *tremendous terror* of their own death or the death of those around them,
- a strong *desire not to stand out* or be different,
- *fear* of going to sleep, and/or
- *revenge* that can manifest in very aggressive behavior.

Educators can help by doing the following:

1.  Telling faculty, students, parents, and extended community the facts about what happened.  Everyone needs to know the truth as a way of dispelling fear that is so all-pervasive at these times.   Thorough information is important even if it is violent.  It provides a concrete base to work with the uncertainty of what has happened.  If a uniform, clear picture is presented, it will help alleviate hearsay and rumors to which children are exposed.

2.  Acknowledging the tremendous fear associated with violent crimes.  Adults and children become more fearful for their lives and the lives of loved ones.  Anxiety is created about the inability to be protected by anyone in the adult world.

3.  Suggesting ways to help reduce this fear and anxiety in the school and community environment that allow everyone to feel more secure.

- Carpool
- Neighborhood watch
- Extra security police
- Buddy systems walking home or to the car
- Whistles
- Walkie-talkies on the playground
     (suggested by the Dougy Center, Portland, OR)

**School Crisis Team**

A school-based crisis team is necessary to create added support for the extra responsibilities of media coverage and criminal prosecution.

## ABUSE

Important procedures in abuse prevention include stressing to children certain major points:

- It is not the child's fault.
- A child has the right to say no to anything that or anyone who makes the child feel too uncomfortable or scared.
- Children need to learn ways to tell others in their family or out side of the family what is happening to them.
- Children need practice in role-playing potentially dangerous situations. Teach them to yell or use a whistle if necessary.
- Children need an adult advocate and confidant whom they can trust. Help them decide on two or three adults with whom they feel they can really talk and provide their names and telephone numbers.
- If something is happening to children or a friend that seems scary or disgusting, children should tell this trusted adult who can help stop it.

Educators can help by doing the following:

- Providing programs that give children the courage and the tools to tell about abuse. These tools include recognition of danger signals and enhancement of confidence.
- Creating school-based prevention programs that include parents. These programs can help parents talk to their children about abuse and provide understanding of ways to help their children prevent the abuse.
- Reporting suspected abuse to Health and Rehabilitative Services (HRS) in individual states or calling Childhelp USA at 1-800-422-4453.

## WHAT CAN EDUCATORS DO ABOUT ABUSE?

1. Role-play with children: What would you do if . . . ? How would you say no if . . . ?
2. Create positive storytelling. Create a story about some type of abuse and provide a safe and positive outcome.
3. Teach children their name, address, and telephone number. Teach them not to give this information to strangers.
4. Provide a preventive resource library. Books include vocabulary that allows children to feel powerful and positive solutions to abusive situations.
5. Encourage physical activity. Children gain confidence that they can protect themselves.

## RESOURCES SPECIFICALLY FOR EDUCATORS

Kathleen Cassini and Jacqueline Rogers (1990) wrote *Death and the Classroom.* This is a teacher's guide that provides practical suggestions for helping the bereaved student.

Majel Gliko-Braden (1992) wrote *Grief Comes to Class.* The purpose of this book is to help teachers work with bereaved children.

*A Student Dies, A School Mourns . . . Are You Prepared?*, by Ralph Klicker (1990), helps prepare educators for a death in the school community. It offers ways to assist the school in creating and implementing a crisis response plan.

*Suicide Prevention in Schools,* by Antoon Leenaars and Susanne Wenckstern (1991), presents facts on today's suicide occurrences in children and adolescents and prevention, intervention, and postvention that can be used effectively in schools.

*Death: In the School Community,* by Martha Oates (1993), is a handbook for counselors, teachers, and administrators to help provide the right words and actions to help students cope with death.

*Growing Through Grief,* by Donna O'Toole (1989), is an excellent resource that provides a well-organized and thought out K-12 curriculum for helping children work through their loss and grief.

*Suicide Prevention,* by Judie Smith (1989), presents a crisis intervention curriculum for teenagers and young adults. It includes attitudes about suicide, suicide information, warning signs, communication skills, and crisis intervention and community resources.

*Good Grief,* by Barbara Ward (1993), is a manual that explores feelings, loss, and death for children under 11. It provides insight as to what to do when a child in school is bereaved.

## THE CAP PROJECT

The Child Assault Prevention (CAP) Project is a comprehensive prevention program offering children's workshops, parents' workshops, and teacher/staff in-service workshops to help prevent verbal, physical, and sexual assaults on children.

CAP Project National Office
P.O. Box 02084
Columbus, OH 43202
(614) 291-2540

# PART IV
# RESOURCES

# Chapter 9

## NATIONAL RESOURCES BRIDGE THE GAP

■ Networking ■ Research ■ Hotlines
■ Information ■ Organizations

# CHILDREN'S GRIEF AND LOSS RESOURCES

Mental health agencies
Child advocate programs
Hospice programs
Hospital bereavement programs
Funeral service professionals
Pediatricians
Clergy
School counselors
School psychologists
Pupil personnel workers
Nurses
Agencies or programs dealing with specific
   losses
Hotlines

## HOTLINES

National AIDS Hotline
1-800-342-AIDS

National Coalition Against Domestic Violence
1-800-333-7233

Child Abuse Hotline
1-800-4ACHILD
1-800-2ACHILD (TDD for Hearing
Impaired)

Food Addiction Hotline
1-800-872-0088

Grief Recovery Hotline
1-800-445-4808

National Center for Missing & Exploited Children
1-800-843-5678

Fathers and Children's Rights Hotline
1-800-843-5678

Parents Anonymous
1-800-421-0352

## CRISIS INTERVENTION FOR CHILDREN AND TEENAGERS

Boys Town Crisis Hotline
1-800-448-3000

Covenant House Hotline
1-800-999-9999

Kid Save
1-800-543-7283

National Runaway and Suicide Hotline
1-800-621-4000

# RESOURCES FOR SUICIDE

American Association of Suicidology
4201 Connecticut Avenue, Suite 310
Washington, DC 20008
202-237-2280

Samaritans (Suicide)
500 Commonwealth Avenue
Boston, MA 02215
617-247-0220 (24 hours)
617-247-8050 (teens)

Suicide Education and Information Center
723 Fourteenth Street,NW, #102
Calgary, Alberta
Canada T2N 2A4
403-283-3031

Suicide Information and Education Centre
  (SIEC)
201,16165 - 10th Avenue, SW
Calgary, Alberta
Canada T3C 0J7
403-245-3900

Suicide Prevention and Crisis Service of
  Tompkins County, Inc.
P.O. Box 312
Ithaca, NY 14851
607-272-1505

Suicide Prevention Center, Inc.
P.O. Box 1393
Dayton, OH 45401-1393
513-297-9096

Suicide Research Unit
National Institute of Mental Health
5600 Fishers Lane, Room 10C26
Rockville, MD 20857

Youth Resource Service
P.O. Box 2100
Manhasset, NY 11030

Youth Suicide National Center
1825 Eye Street, NW, #400
Washington, DC  20006
202-429-2016

# RESOURCES FOR VIOLENCE AND HOMICIDE

American Bar Association
Victim/Witness Program
1800 M Street, NW
Washington, DC  20036
202-331-2260

American Trauma Society
1400 Mercantile Lane, Suite #188
Landover, MD 20785
1-800-556-7890

Crime Victims Litigation Project
c/o National Victim Center
4530 Ocean Front
Virginia Beach, VA 23451
804-422-2692

Mothers Against Drunk Driving (MADD)
669 Airport Freeway, Suite 310
Hurst, TX 76053
1-800-633-6233

NOVA (National Organization for Victim
  Assistance)
717 D Street, NW
Washington, DC  20004
202-393-NOVA

National Sheriffs Association Victim
  Program
1450 Duke Street
Alexandria, VA 22314
703-836-7837
1-800-424-7827

National Victim Center
307 W 7th Street, Suite 1001
Fort Worth, TX 76102
817-877-3355

National Victim's Resource Center
P. O. Box 6000 AIQ
Rockville, MD 20850
1-800-627-NVRC

Office for Victims of Crime
633 Indiana Avenue, NW
Washington, DC 20531
202-724-5947

Parents of Murdered Children
1739 Bella Vista
Cincinnati, OH  45237
513-721-LOVE

Tragedy Assistance Program for Survivors, Inc.
807 G Street, Suite 250
Anchorage, AK 99501
1-800-959-TAPS

Victims of Crime Resource Center
McGeorge School of Law
University of the Pacific
3200 Fifth Avenue
Sacramento, CA 95817
1-800-VICTIMS

## RESOURCES FOR AIDS

AIDS Action Committee
131 Clarendon Street
Boston, MA 02116
617-536-7733 (Hotline)
617-437-6200

AIDS Atlanta
1132 W Peachtree Street, NW, Suite 102
Atlanta, GA 30309
1-800-342-2437

The AIDS Health Project
P.O. Box 0884
San Francisco, CA 94143
415-476-6430

AIDS Resource Center
National PTA
700 North Rush Street
Chicago, IL 60611
415-476-6430

America for a Sound AIDS Policy (ASAP)
P.O. Box 17433
Washington, DC  20041
703-471-7350

American Academy of Child and Adolescent
Psychiatry Committee on HIV Issues
3615 Wisconsin Avenue, NW
Washington, DC 20016
202-966-7300

American Academy of Pediatrics
Committee on School Health
141 NW Point Boulevard
P. O. Box 297
Elk Grove Village, IL 60009-0927
1-800-433-9016

American Foundation for AIDS Research
1515 Broadway, Suite 3601
New York, NY 10032
212-719-0033

American Red Cross
AIDS Education Office
1709 New York Avenue, NW
Washington, DC 20006
202-434-4074

Association for the Care of Children's Health
3615 Wisconsin Avenue, NW
Washington, DC 20016
202-654-6549

Health Education Resource Organization
 (HERO)
101 West Read Street, Suite 812
Baltimore, MD 21203
301-685-1180

March of Dimes
Birth Defect Foundation
1275 Mamaroneck Avenue
White Plains, NY 10805
914-428-7100

National AIDS Information Clearinghouse
P.O. Box 6003
Rockville, MD 20850
1-800-458-5231

National Association for Children with AIDS
P.O. Box 15485
Durham, NC  27704
919-477-5288

Pan American Health Organization/WHO
AIDS Program
525 23rd Street, NW
Washington, DC  20037
202-861-4346

Pediatric AIDS Network
Children's Hospital of Los Angeles
4650 Sunset Boulevard, Box 55
Los Angeles, CA 90027
213-669-5616

San Francisco AIDS Foundation
P.O. Box 6182
San Francisco, CA 94101
415-861-3397

SIECUS
Sex Information and Education
  Council of the U.S.
130 West 42nd Street, Suite 2500
New York, NY 10036
212-819-9770

## RESOURCES FOR ABUSE

American Association for Protecting
  Children
c/o American Humane Society
63 Inverness Drive, East
Englewood, CO 80112-5117
303-792-9900

Child Assault Prevention (CAP)
  National Office
P.O. Box 02084
Columbus, OH 43202
614-291-2540

Childhelp IOS Foresters
P.O. Box 630
Hollywood, CA 90028
1-800-4ACHILD (Hotline)
1-800-2ACHILD (TDD for hearing impaired)


International Society of Prevention of Child
  Abuse and Neglect
1205 Oneida Street
Denver, CO  80220
303-321-3963

National Resource Center on Child
  Sexual Abuse
107 Lincoln Street
Huntsville, AL  35801
205-534-6868

Parents Anonymous, National Headquarters
22330 Hawthorne Boulevard, Suite 208
Torrance, CA 90505
1-800-421-1325

# NATIONAL RESOURCES AND ORGANIZATIONS

Advocates for Children and Youth, Inc.
300 Cathedral Street, Suite 500
Baltimore, MD 21201
410-547-9200

Association for the Care of Children's Health
7910 Woodmont Avenue
Bethesda, MD 20814
301-654-6549

Association for Death Education and
  Counseling (ADEC)
639 Prospect Avenue
Hartford, CT 06105
203-232-4285

Boarder Baby Project
2201 Wisconsin Avenue, NW, Suite 330
Washington, DC 20007
202-333-6500

The Candlelighters
1312 18th Street, NW
Washington, DC 20036
202-659-5136

Center for Loss and Grief Therapy
10400 Connecticut Avenue, Suite 514
Kensington, MD 20895
301-942-6440

Center for Loss and Life Transition
3735 Broken Arrow Road
Fort Collins, CO 80526
303-226-6050

Children of Separation and Divorce
2000 Century Plaza, #121
Columbia, MD  21044
410-740-9553

Children's Hospice International
11011 King Street, Suite 131
Alexandria, VA 22314
703-556-042

Compassionate Friends, Inc.
National Headquarters
P.O. Box 1347
Oak Brook, IL 60521
312-323-5010

Dougy's Place
P.O. Box 86852
Portland, OR 97286
503-775-5683

Down Syndrome Society
666 Broadway, Suite 810
New York, NY 10012
1-800-221-2402

The Good Grief Program
Judge Baker Guidance Center
295 Longwood Avenue
Boston, MA 02115
617-232-8390

Hospice Education Institute
P.O. Box 713
Essex, CT 06426-0713
1-800-331-1620 (Computerized "Hospice
  Link")

Inner Source
980 Awald Drive
Annapolis, MD  21403
410-269-6298

Institute for Attitudinal Studies
P.O. Box 19222
Alexandria, VA 22320
703-706-5333

Kids and Crisis
P.O. Box 3201
Center Line, MI 48015
810-557-6089

National Hospice Organization
1901 N. Fort Myer Drive
Arlington, VA 22209
703-243-5900

National Sudden Infant Death Syndrome
  Foundation
105000 Little Patuxent Parkway, Suite 420
Columbia, MD  21044
1-800-221-SIDS

Parent Encouragement Center (PEP)
10100 Connecticut Avenue
Kensington, MD 20895
301-929-8824

Parents Without Partners
7910 Woodmont Avenue, Suite 1000
Bethesda, MD 20814
1-800-638-8078

Pregnancy and Infant Loss Center
1421 E Wayzata Boulevard, Suite 30
Wayzata, MN 55391
612-473-9372

(formerly Resolve Thru Sharing)
Bereavement Services/RTS
Gunderson Lutheran Medical Center
1910 South Avenue
Lacrosse, WI 54601
608-791-4747
1-800-362-9567, ext. 4747

Ronald McDonald House
419 E 86th Street
New York, NY 10028
212-876-1590

Share Pregnancy & Infant Loss
St. Joseph's Health Center
300 First Capitol Drive
St. Charles, MO 63301
314-947-6164

Sibling Support Center
4800 Sand Point Way, NE
P.O. Box C5371
Seattle, WA 98105

St. Francis Center
5135 MacArthur Boulevard, NW
Washington, DC 20016
202-363-8500

Stephen Daniel Jeffreys Foundation, Ltd.
Grief Counseling Service
c/o Family Life Center
Wilde Lake Village Green
Columbia, MD 21044
410-997-4884

**Chapter 10**

# MATERIALS TO EXPLORE AND ANNOTATED BIBLIOGRAPHY: THERE IS HOPE

■ Books ■ Videos ■ Manuals
■ Guides ■ Curricula

## ADULT RESOURCES THAT HELP

### Books for Adults

Bolton, I. (1983). *My Son . . . My Son . . .* Atlanta, GA: Bolton Press. Iris Bolton's personal story of her son's suicide is deeply moving and revealing.

Bothum, L. (1988). *When Friends Ask About Adoption.* Chevy Chase, MD: Swan Publications. A useful question-and-answer guide on adoption for caring adults and nonadoptive parents.

Bradshaw, J. (1988). *The Family: A Revolutionary Way of Self-Discovery.* Deerfield Beach, FL: Health Communications. An introspective view of family systems and inner child work.

Brett, D. (1986). *Annie Stories.* New York, NY: Workman Publishing. A series of stories that can be read to children under 10 dealing with many childhood issues, such as death and divorce. The author provides advice for caring adults on how to use these stories.

Capacchione, L. (1989). *The Creative Journal for Children.* Boston, MA: Shambhala. This is a creative journal that provides ways for caring adults to help children express their thoughts and feelings.

Cassini, K., & Rogers, J. (1990). *Death and the Classroom.* Cincinnati, OH: Griefwork of Cinncinnati. A text that confronts death in the classroom.

Celotta, B. (1991). *Generic Crisis Intervention Procedures.* Gaithersburg, MD: Beverly Celotta Publisher. A guide for youth suicide crisis intervention in school settings.

Coles, R. (1991). *The Spiritual Life of Children.* Boston, MA: Houghton Mifflin. A book sharing thoughts, drawings, and dreams that reflect the inner world of children.

Dass, R., & Gorman, P. (1985). *How Can I Help?* New York, NY: Alfred A. Knopf. A book of stories and reflections on service and how we can help with a loving heart.

Douglas, G. (1995). *Dead Opposite.* New York, NY: Henry Holt and Co. A compelling account of the murder of a well loved Yale student and the 16-year-old gang member accused of the murder.

DuPrau, J. (1981). *Adoption.* New York, NY: Julian Mesner. A series of different stories for young adults about facts and feelings related to adoption. It includes a list of helpful agencies.

Fitzgerald, H. (1992). *The Grieving Child.* New York, NY: Simon and Schuster. A wonderful guide for parents to use to help children work with their grief.

Fitzgerald, H. (1994). *The Mourning Handbook.* New York, NY: Simon and Schuster. This is a comprehensive and compassionate resource to help families cope with death and dying. It explores complicated grief, murder, and suicide.

Fox, S. (1988). *Good Grief: Helping Groups of Children When a Friend Dies.* Boston, MA: New England Association for the Education of Young Children. An excellent source of information for adults working with children whose friends have died.

Frankl, V. (1984). *Man's Search for Meaning.* New York, NY: Simon and Schuster. A powerful account of the author's imprisonment in Nazi Germany and the love that helped him survive his losses.

Furth, G. (1988). *The Secret World of Drawings.* Boston, MA: Sigo Press. A comprehensive look at children's artwork and ways of understanding it.

Galinsky, E., & David, J. (1988). *The Preschool Years.* New York, NY: Ballantine Books. This book contains a wealth of knowledge for parents and educators on children ages 2 to 5.

Gardner, S. (1990). *Teenage Suicide.* Englewood Cliffs, NJ: Prentice-Hall. This book examines some of the reasons and causes of teenage suicide and offers some solutions.

Gibran, K. (1969). *The Prophet.* New York, NY: Alfred A. Knopf. A beautiful book of poetry expressing timeless feelings of life and death, pleasure and pain, and joy and sorrow.

Gil, E. (1991). *The Healing Power of Play.* New York, NY: Guilford Publisher. This book gives a history of play therapy and specific considerations for working with abused and neglected children.

Ginsberg, H., & Opper, S. (1976). *Piaget's Theory of Intellectual Development.* Englewood Cliffs, NJ: Prentice-Hall. A thorough look at Piaget's theory of development.

Gliko-Braden, M. (1992). *Grief Comes to Class.* Omaha, NE: Centering Corporation. This book is meant to help teachers and parents assist bereaved children.

Golden, T. (1994). *A Man's Grief.* Kensington, MD: Tom Golden. Tom Golden has written an excellent series of pamphlets on men and grief. They define grief for men, describe gender differences, and offer ways men can work with their grief.

Goldman, L. (1994). *Life and Loss: A Guide to Help Grieving Children.* Muncie, IN: Accelerated Development. A book that explains clearly and simply children's loss and grief issues and ways that caring adults can help.

Grollman, E. (1967). *Explaining Death to Children.* Boston, MA: Beacon Press. A book geared to adults who want to ease a child's first confrontation with the death of a loved one.

Heavilin, M. (1986). *Roses in December.* San Bernardino, CA: Here's Life Publishers. The author expresses a deep understanding of the grieving process, having experienced the death of three children.

Hendriks, J., Black, D., & Kaplan, T. (1993). *When Father Kills Mother.* New York, NY: Routledge. The authors combine their knowledge of bereavement and posttraumatic stress disorder to help children who have witnessed extreme violence.

Huntley, T. (1991). *Helping Children Grieve When Someone They Love Dies.* Minneapolis, MN: Augsburg Fortress. An easy to read resource for caring adults that addresses children's grief honestly.

Ilse, S. (1982). *Empty Arms.* Maple Plain, MN: Wintergreen Press. This is a practical book for anyone who has experienced infant death or miscarriage. It offers suggestions and support for decision making at the time of loss and future concerns and grief work.

Johnson, S. (1987). *After a Child Dies: Counseling Bereaved.* New York, NY: Springer Publishing. A comprehensive text that offers information on counseling bereaved families when a child dies.

Kubler-Ross, E. (1975). *On Death and Dying.* Englewood Cliffs, NJ: Prentice-Hall. A pioneering book on the subject of death and dying, using real-life situations to create true understanding.

Kubler-Ross, E. (1985). *On Children and Dying.* New York, NY: Macmillan. Elisabeth Kubler-Ross offers families of dead and dying children honest information, helpful ideas, and strength to cope.

Kushner, H. (1981). *When Bad Things Happen to Good People.* New York, NY: Avon Books. Rabbi Kushner shares his thoughts and feelings of why we suffer. The book was written following his son's illness and subsequent death.

Leenaars, A., & Wenckstern, S. (1990). *Suicide Prevention in Schools.* New York, NY: Hemisphere. The authors attempt to outline the state of the art of suicide prevention in schools.

Leon, I. (1990). *When a Baby Dies.* New Haven, CT: Yale University Press. The first book to explore therapeutically the loss of a baby during pregnancy or as a newborn. It addresses the subject of surviving siblings.

Levine, S. (1987). *Healing into Life and Death.* New York, NY: Anchor Press. Stephen Levine explores ways to open our hearts to healing.

Linn, E. (1990). *150 Facts About Grieving Children.* Incline Village, NV: The Publisher's Mark. A series of 150 paragraphs discussing important information and understandings about the grieving child.

Livingston, G. (1995). *Only Spring: On Mourning the Death of My Son.* New York: HarperCollins. An inspiring story of a father's love for his 6-year-old son, Lucus, and his deeply moving journey through his child's illness and death.

Lord, J. (1993). *No Time for Goodbyes.* Ventura, CA: Pathfinder Publishing. This book provides important suggestions for survivors grieving a loved one who has been killed.

MacLean, G. (1990). *Suicide in Children and Adolescents.* Lewiston, NY: Hogrefe & Huber Publishers. A practical and hands-on guide to work with children and young people at risk of killing themselves.

McEvoy, M., & McEvoy, A. (1994). *Preventing Youth Suicide*. Holmes Beach, FL: Learning Publications. This is a powerful handbook for educators and human service professionals to help prevent youth suicide.

Middelton-Moz, J. (1989). *Children of Trauma*. Deerfield Beach, FL: Health Communications. *Children of Trauma* helps the reader discover his or her discarded self by coming face-to-face with emotional fears that may be the result of a traumatic childhood.

Middleton-Moz, J., & Swinell, L. (1986). *After the Tears*. Deerfield Beach, FL: Health Communications. This book helps adults come to terms with childhood trauma involving alcoholism.

Miller, A. (1984). *For Your Own Good*. New York, NY: Farrar, Straus, and Giroux. Alice Miller explores deeply the repercussions of adults taking over a child's will.

Mills, G., Reisler, R., Robinson, A., & Vermilye, G. (1976). *Discussing Death*. Palm Springs, CA: ETC Publications. A guide for death education giving practical suggestions and resources for many age levels.

Moustakas, C. (1992). *Psychotherapy with Children*. Greeley, CO: Carron. A classic text in understanding the therapeutic environment. This book creates guidelines and practical techniques to use when working with children in psychotherapy.

Oaklander, V. (1969). *Windows to Our Children: Gestalt Therapy for Children*. New York, NY: Center for Gestalt Development. A Gestalt Therapy approach to children's loss and grief work with stories and practical suggestions for play therapy.

Peck, S. (1978). *The Road Less Traveled*. New York, NY: Simon and Schuster. Scott Peck explores traditional values and spiritual growth through a psychology of love.

Quackenbush, J., & Graveline, D. (1985). *When Your Pet Dies.* New York, NY: Pocket Books. A book for pet owners to help understand feelings when a pet dies.

Rando, T. (1988). *How to Go on Living When Someone You Love Dies.* New York, NY: Lexington Books. A helpful and informative book addressing grief and how to work with it.

Redmond, L. (1990). *Surviving When Someone You Love Was Murdered.* Clearwater, FL: Psychological Consultation and Educational Services. This is a professional's guide to group therapy for families and friends of murder victims.

Roberts, J., & Johnson, J. (1994). *Thank You for Coming to Say Good-bye.* Omaha, NE: Centering Corporation. For parents, funeral directors, and other caring professionals to help suggest ways to involve children in funeral services.

Sandefer, K. (1990). *Mom, I'm All Right.* Garretson, SD: Sanders Printing. This is a book for parents and caring professionals addressing teen suicide. It is a mother's own story about her child's suicide and advice and warnings she feels are helpful.

Sanders, C. (1992). *How to Survive the Loss of a Child.* Rocklin, CA: Prima Publishing. This book helps explain the phases of grief for the bereaved parent and offers help in understanding the process of healing through grief.

Shamos, T., & Patros, P. (1990). *"I Want to Kill Myself."* Lexington, MA: Lexington Books. This book talks frankly about children who are seriously depressed, signs to watch for, and ways to help.

Siegel, B. (1986). *Love, Medicine and Miracles.* New York, NY: Harper and Row. A book that emphasizes recognizing how our mind influences our body and how to use that knowledge for healing.

Smilansky, S. (1987). *On Death (Helping Children Understand and Cope).* New York, NY: Peter Lang. The author bases her studies on children and their grief processes in Tel Aviv.

Stillion, J., & McDowell, E. (1996). *Suicide Across the Lifespan—Premature Exits, Second Edition.* Washington, DC: Taylor & Francis. This book is designed for graduate and undergraduate college students to help them examine developmental principles applying to suicide.

Trout, S. (1990). *To See Differently.* Washington, DC: Three Roses Press. This is an excellent book to help readers heal their minds after facing many life issues. A chapter on working with feelings about death is included.

Webb, N. B. (1993). *Helping Bereaved Children.* New York, NY: The Guilford Press. This text contains theory, illustrative cases, and practical examples that professionals can use when working with bereaved children.

Wolfelt, A. (1983). *Helping Children Cope with Grief.* Muncie, IN: Accelerated Development. An informative resource for caring adults working with bereaved children. Includes ideas for leading discussions.

Wolfelt, A. (1992). *Sarah's Journey.* Fort Collins, CO: Center for Loss and Life Transition. Eight-year-old Sarah's father suddenly died. Wolfelt presents 3 years of Sarah's grief experience and provides counseling perspectives and guidelines for caring adults.

Worden, J. W. (1991). *Grief Counseling and Grief Therapy.* New York, NY: Springer. A comprehensive handbook for grief counseling.

**Videos for Adults**

Kathleen, B. (1994). *To Touch a Grieving Heart.* Salt Lake City, UT: Panacom Video Publishing. This film has very sensitive and practical insights into helping families with grief.

Wolfelt, A. (1991). *A Child's View of Grief.* Fort Collins, CO: Center for Loss and Life Transition. A 20-minute video with children and parents sharing real stories and emotions.

Research Press. (1989). *A Family in Grief: The Ameche Story.* Champagne, IL: Research Press. A real family story of bereavement, with guide included.

Dougy Center. (1992). *Dougy's Place: A 20-20 Video.* Portland, OR: Dougy Center. A candid look at the kids participating in the Dougy Center's program.

Kussman, L. (1992). *What Do I Tell My Children?* Wellesley, MA: Aquarian Productions. A film narrated by Joanne Woodward showing experts, adults, and children exploring their thoughts and feelings regarding death.

Ebeling, C., & Ebeling, D. (1991). *When Grief Comes to School.* Bloomington, IN: Blooming Educational Enterprises. A film and manual showing families and school personnel discussing grief issues.

## Videos for Children

O'Toole D. (1994). *Aarvy Aardvark Finds Hope.* Burnsville, NC: Mt. Rainbow Publications. The incredible journey of Aarvy Aardvark and the grief he experiences is presented through puppets and music for young children to relate to and learn from.

Rogers, F. (1993). *Mr. Rogers Talks About Living and Dying.* Pittsburgh, PA: Family Communications Inc. This is a warm and comforting video that presents answers to questions about living and dying.

## Curricula and Manuals

Celotta, B. (1991). *Generic Crisis Intervention Procedures.* Gaithersburg, MD: Celotta. A practical manual for youth suicide crisis intervention in schools.

Cunningham, L. (1990). *Teen Age Grief (TAG).* Panorama City, CA: Teen Age Grief. An excellent training manual for initiating grief support groups for teens.

Davis, N. (1990). *Once Upon a Time.* Oxon Hill, MD: Psychological Associates of Oxon Hill. One of the best manuals I have seen, this book provides therapeutic stories for children with a guide for each story. Covers a wide range of topics including all abuses and death.

Garon, R., DeLeonardis, G., & Mandell, B. (1993). *Guidelines for Child Focused Decision Making.* Columbia, MD: The Children of Separation and Divorce. An exceptional manual for judges, attorneys, mediators, and mental health professionals concerning children and divorce.

Kirsh, A., Cobb, S., & Curley, S. (1991). *Plan of Action for Helping Schools Deal with Death and Dying.* Center Line, MI: The Kids In Crisis Program. An excellent protocol for schools working with kids in crisis when death or dying occurs.

Klicker, R. (1990). *A Student Dies, A School Mourns . . . Are You Prepared?* Buffalo, NY: Thanos Institute. This manual guides the school community in reducing the effects of personal loss and suffering when death occurs.

Lagorio, J. (1991). *Life Cycle Education Manual.* Solana Beach, CA: Empowerment in Action. A teacher's guide to help with loss issues including specific lesson plans and guided book activities.

O'Toole, D. (1989). *Growing Through Grief.* Burnsville, NC: Mt. Rainbow Publications. A K-12 curriculum to help children through loss.

Smith, J. (1989). *Suicide Prevention.* Holmes Beach, FL: Learning Publications. A crisis intervention curriculum that provides a school-based program for teenagers on suicide prevention.

## Book Services

Centering Corporation. Omaha, NE. A comprehensive grief resource center created by Marv and Joy Johnson offering publications, workshops, and membership programs on all aspects of loss and grief. 402-553-1200.

Child'swork/Child'splay. King of Prussia, PA. A catalog that addresses the mental health needs of children, parents, and counselors.

Compassion Book Service and Mt. Rainbow Publications. Burnsville, NC. A wealth of resources and training tools are provided by Donna O'Toole that include books, videos, and audio cassettes dealing with loss, death, dying, bereavement, comfort, and hope. 704-675-9687.

Mar*co Products, Incorporated. Warminster, PA. A resource made for and made by educators that provides materials for professionals working with elementary, middle, and high school age children. 1-800-448-2197.

Waterfront Books Publishing. Burlington, VT. A service offering books that support children and the adults in their lives.

Wintergreen Press. Maple Plain, MN. A resource for materials relating to grief associated with miscarriage, stillbirth, and infant death.

## Tapes for Children and Teenagers

Cunningham, L. (1993). *Teen Grief*. Newhall, CA:  Teen Age Grief.  Teenagers give personal interviews about their grief and loss experiences.  For teens.

Hoffman, J. (1985). *Children's Meditation Tape.*  Shawnee Mission, KS: Rythmic Mission.  A child's tape of relaxation games and guided imagery.  Ages 2 to 11.

## CHILDREN'S RESOURCES THAT HELP

### Books for Children About Death

Brown, M. W. (1979). *The Dead Bird.*  New York, NY:  Dell Publishing.  A story of four children who find a dead bird, bury it, and hold a funeral service. Ages 4 to 8.

Campbell, J. A. (1992). *The Secret Places.*  Omaha, NE:  Centering Corporation.  The story of Ryan and his journey through grief is for children and adults to gain an in-depth look at childhood grief.  Ages 6 to 12.

Dodge, N. (1984). *Thumpy's Story: The Story of Grief and Loss Shared by Thumpy the Bunny.*  Springfield, IL:  Prairie Lark Press.  The story of the death of Thumpy's sister, who was not strong enough to keep living.  Ages 5 to 12.

Ferguson, D. (1992). *A Bunch of Balloons.*  Omaha, NE:  Centering Corporation.  A resource to help grieving children understand loss and remember what they have left after someone dies.  Ages 5 to 8.

Oehler, J. (1978). *The Frog Family's Baby Dies*. Durham, NC: Duke University Medical Center.  A coloring story book for very young children discussing sibling loss.  Ages 3 to 6.

O'Toole, D. (1988). *Aarvy Ardvark Finds Hope* (adult manual available).  Burnsville, NC: Mt. Rainbow Publications.  The story of animals that presents pain, sadness, and eventual hope after death.  Ages 5 to 8.

Scravani, M. (1988). *Love, Mark*. Syracuse, NY: Hope for Bereaved. Letters written by grieving children to help them express feelings. Ages 7 to 12.

Stein, S. (1974). *About Dying*. New York, NY: Walker and Co. Simple text and photographs to help young children understand death, including a discussion about children's feelings for adults. Ages 3 to 6.

Varley, S. (1984). *Badger's Parting Gifts*. New York, NY: Morrow and Co. Badger was a special friend to all the animals. After his death, each friend recalls a special memory of Badger. All ages.

White, E. B. (1952). *Charlotte's Web*. New York, NY: Harper and Row. Through the eyes of the farm animals, life and death are sweetly portrayed. Ages 8 to 13.

## Books for Teenagers About Death

Bode, J. (1993). *Death Is Hard to Live With*. New York, NY: Bantam Doubleday Dell Publishing. Teenagers talk frankly about how they cope with loss.

Dorfman, E. (1994). *The C-Word*. Portland, OR: New Sage Press. This author battled her own cancer at 16 and her mother's death due to breast cancer. Dorfman interviews five teenagers and their families sharing their cancer experiences.

Gootman, M. (1994). *When a Friend Dies*. Minneapolis, MN: Free Spirit Publishing. This book was inspired by a mom who watched her teenage children suffer over the loss of a friend. It helps teens recognize and validate their feelings and provides good suggestions for healing.

Kolf, J. C. (1990). *Teenagers Talk About Grief*. Grand Rapids, MI: Baker Book House. A book written especially for and about teenage grief with accounts of firsthand experiences.

## Book About Grieving

Spies, K. (1993). *Everything You Need to Know About Grieving*. New York, NY: The Rosen Publishing Co. This book helps explain how kids can talk to other kids who are going through a grief process. Ages 7 to 12.

## Book About a Parent Dying

McNamara, J. (1994). *My Mom Is Dying.* Minneapolis, MN: Augsburg Fortress. This book is a diary by Kristine, a young girl who learns her mom is dying. It includes a discussion section for parents. Ages 5 to 9.

## Books About Death of a Parent

Blume, J. (1981). *Tiger Eyes.* New York, NY: Macmillan Children's Group. Fifteen-year-old Davey works through the feelings of his father's murder in a store holdup. Ages 11 and up.

Douglas, E. (1990). *Rachel and the Upside Down Heart.* Los Angeles, CA: Price Stern Sloan. The true story of 4-year-old Rachel and how her father's death affects her life. Ages 5 to 9.

Frost, D. (1991). *DAD! Why'd You Leave Me?* Scottdale, PA: Herald Press. This is a story about 10-year-old Ronnie who cannot understand why his dad died. Ages 8 to 12.

Greenfield, E. (1993). *Nathanial Talking.* New York, NY: Black Butterfly Children's Group. Nathanial, an energetic 9-year-old, helps us understand a black child's world after his mom dies. He uses rap and rhyme to express his feelings. Ages 7 to 11.

Krementz, J. (1983). *How It Feels When a Parent Dies.* New York, NY: Knopf. Eighteen children (ages 7 to 16) speak openly about their feelings and experiences after the death of a parent.

Lanton, S. (1991). *Daddy's Chair.* Rockville, MD: Kar-Ben Copies. Michael's dad died. The book follows the Shiva, the Jewish week of mourning. Michael doesn't want anyone to sit in Daddy's chair. Ages 5 to 10.

LeShan, E. (1975). *Learning to Say Goodbye When a Parent Dies.* New York, NY: Macmillan. Written directly to children about problems to be recognized and overcome when a parent dies. Ages 8 and up.

Lowden, S. (1993). *Emily's Sadhappy Season.* Omaha, NE: Centering Corporation. The story of a young girl's feelings after her father dies. Ages 6 to 10.

Powell, E. S. (1990). *Geranium Morning.* Minneapolis, MN: Carol Rhoda Books. A boy's dad is killed in a car accident and a girl's mom is dying. The children share their feelings. Ages 6 and up.

Thaut, P. (1991). *Spike and Ben.* Deerfield Beach, FL: Health Communications. The story of a boy whose friend's mom dies. Ages 5 to 8.

Tiffault, B. (1992). *A Quilt for Elizabeth.* Omaha, NE: Centering Corporation. Elizabeth's grandmother helps her understand her feelings after her father dies. This is a good story to initiate an open dialogue with children. Ages 7 and up.

Vigna, J. (1991). *Saying Goodbye to Daddy.* Niles, IL: Albert Whitman and Co. A sensitive story about a dad's death and the healing that takes place in the weeks that follow. Ages 5 to 8.

## Books About Sibling Death

Alexander, S. (1983). *Nadia the Willful.* New York, NY: Pantheon Books. Nadia's older brother dies, and she helps her father heal his grief by willfully talking about her brother. Ages 6 to 10.

Erling, J., & Erling, S. (1986). *Our Baby Died. Why?* Maple Plain, MN: Pregnancy and Infant Loss Center. A little boy shares his feelings about the death of his stillborn brother and eventual birth of sibling twins. Children can read, draw, and color. Ages 4 to 10.

Gryte, M. (1991). *No New Baby.* Omaha, NE: Centering Corporation. Siblings are allowed to express their feelings about Mom's miscarriage. Ages 5 to 8.

Johnson, J., & Johnson, M. (1982). *Where's Jess?* Omaha, NE: Centering Corporation. A book for young children that addresses the questions and feelings kids have when a sibling dies. Ages 4 to 7.

Linn, E. (1982). *Children Are Not Paperdolls.* Springfield, IL: Human Services Press. Kids who have had brothers and sisters die draw and comment on their experiences. Ages 8 to 12.

Richter, E. (1986). *Losing Someone You Love: When a Brother or Sister Dies.* New York, NY: Putnam. Adolescents share feelings and experiences about the death of a sibling. Ages 11 and up.

Romond, J. (1989). *Children Facing Grief.* St. Meinrad, IN: Abbey Press. Letters from bereaved brothers and sisters, telling of their experiences and offering hope. Ages 6 to 14.

Sims, A. (1986). *Am I Still a Sister?* Slidell, LA: Big A and Co. This story was written by an 11-year-old who experienced her baby brother's death. Ages 8 to 12.

Temes, R. (1992). *The Empty Place.* Far Hills, NJ: Small Horizons. The story of a third-grade boy whose older sister dies. Ages 5 to 9.

## Books About a Friend's Death

Blackburn, L. (1987). *Timothy Duck.* Omaha, NE: Centering Corporation. Timothy Duck's friend John gets sick and dies. He shares his feelings. Ages 5 to 8.

Blackburn, L. (1991). *The Class in Room 44.* Omaha, NE: Centering Corporation. The children in Room 44 share their feelings of grief when their classmate Tony dies. Ages 6 to 10.

Cohen, J. (1987). *I Had a Friend Named Peter.* New York, NY: William Morrow and Co. Betsy's friend Peter dies suddenly. She learns through parents and teachers that Peter's memory can live on. Ages 5 to 10.

Kaldhol, M., & Wenche, O. (1987). *Goodbye Rune.* New York, NY: Kane-Miller. A story about the drowning death of a girl's best friend and how parents can help. Ages 5 to 12.

Kubler-Ross, E. (1987). *Remember the Secret.* Berkeley, CA: Celestial Arts. The imaginative story of love and faith of two children and their experience with death. Ages 5 to 10.

## Books About Death of a Grandparent

Fassler, J. (1983). *My Grandpa Died Today.* Springfield, IL: Human Sciences Press. David did not fear death as much because Grandpa knew that David would have the courage to live. Ages preschool to 7.

Holden, L. D. (1989). *Gran-Gran's Best Trick.* New York, NY: Magination Press. This book deals directly with cancer. It follows the treatment, sickness, and death of a grandparent. Ages 6 to 12.

Pomerantz, B. (1983). *Bubby, Me, and Memories.* New York, NY: Union of American Hebrew Congregations. A child's grandmother dies. His feelings are addressed and his questions answered. Good source to explain Jewish rituals. Ages 5 to 8.

Thomas, J. (1988). *Saying Goodbye to Grandma.* New York, NY: Clarion Books. A sensitively written book about a family's joining together for Grandma's funeral. Ages 5 to 10.

Thornton, T. (1987). *Grandpa's Chair.* Portland, OR: Multnomah Press. The story of a small boy's love for his grandfather, his last visit to see him, and his grandfather's eventual death. Ages 4 to 8.

Yolen, J. (1994). *Grandad Bill's Song.* New York, NY: Philomel Books. A little boy asks, "What do you do on the day your grandfather dies?" and family and friends talk about memories. Then the boy discovers his own feelings. Ages 5 to 9.

## Workbooks About Death

Boulden, J., & Boulden, J. (1991). *Saying Goodbye.* Santa Rosa, CA: Boulden Publishing. A bereavement workbook and coloring book for young children. Ages 5 to 8.

Haasl, B., & Marnocha, J. (1990). *Bereavement Support Group Program for Children.* Muncie, IN: Accelerated Development. A step-by-step workbook for children and manual for leader to use in a bereavement group. Ages 8 to 13.

Hammond, J. (1980). *When My Mommy Died* or *When My Daddy Died.* Flint, MI: Cranbrook Publishing. Both workbooks are geared to young children's bereavement work after parent death.

Heegaard, M. (1988). *When Someone Very Special Dies.* Minneapolis, MN: Woodland Press. An excellent workbook that uses artwork and journaling to allow children to work through their grief. A facilitator's manual is available. Ages 5 to 12.

Rogers, F. (1991). *So Much to Think About.* Pittsburgh, PA: Family Communications. An activity book for young children when someone they love has died. Ages 5 to 8.

Traisman, E. S. (1992). *Fire in My Heart, Ice in My Veins.* Omaha, NE: Centering Corporation. A wonderful workbook for teenagers to explore thoughts and feelings and record grief memories. For teenagers.

### Special Memory Book

Chimeric. (1991). *Illustory.* Denver, CO: Author. Kids can write and illustrate their own books that can be sent away and made into hardcover bound books with kids' original text. Ages 5 to 10.

### Books About Life Cycles

Buscaglia, L. (1982). *The Fall of Freddie the Leaf.* Thorofare, NJ: Charles B. Slack Co. The story of the changing seasons as a metaphor for life and death. Ages 4 to 8.

Gerstein, M. (1987). *The Mountains of Tibet.* New York, NY: Harper and Row. The story of a woodcutter's journey from the mountains of Tibet through the universe of endless choices and back to his home again. Ages 7 and up.

Mellonie, B., & Ingpen, R. (1983). *Lifetimes: The Beautiful Way to Explain Death to Children*. New York, NY: Bantam Books. Explains the ongoing life cycle of plants, animals, and people. Ages 3 to 10.

Munsch, R. (1983). *Love You Forever*. Willowdale, Canada: A Firefly Book. A beautiful book for adults and children alike about the continuance of love throughout life. All ages.

Wood, D. (1992). *Old Turtle*. Duluth, MN: Pfeifer-Hamilton. A fable for children and adults that captures the message of peace on earth and oneness with nature. The illustrations are beautiful. Ages 5 and up.

## Book About a Depressed Parent

Sanford, D. (1993). *It Won't Last Forever*. Sisters, OR: Questar Publishers. This is the story of Kristen, a little girl who worries over her mom's ongoing sadness. Explains depression to children. Ages 6 to 10.

## Books About a Parent Committing Suicide

Harper, J. (1993). *Hurting Yourself*. Omaha, NE: Centering Corporation. A pamphlet for teenagers and young adults who have intentionally injured themselves. For teenagers.

Kuklin, S. (1994). *After a Suicide: Young People Speak Up*. New York, NY: G.P. Putnam's Sons. This book addresses young people who are survivors after a parent suicide. For teenagers.

Nelson, R., & Galas, J. (1994). *The Power to Prevent Suicide*. Minneapolis, MN: Free Spirit Publishing. This book appears to be very useful in involving teenagers with suicide prevention. It provides practical suggestions and examples with which teenagers can identify.

Urich, J. (1990). *I Wish I Were in a Lonely Meadow: When a Parent Commits Suicide*. Portland OR: Dougy Center. This book is a compilation of children's own writings about their experiences with a parent's suicide. Ages 9 to 15.

## Books About Homicide

Aub, K. (1995). *Children Are Survivors Too.* Boca Raton, FL: Grief Education Enterprises. This book presents many stories by young children and teenagers on their journey as homicide survivors. Ages 6 through teens.

Henry-Jenkins, W. (1993). *Just Us.* Omaha, NE: Centering Corporation. This is a book for teenagers and young adults to help them understand and overcome homicidal loss and grief. For teenagers and young adults.

Mahon, K. L. (1992). *Just One Tear.* New York, NY: Lothrop, Lee, and Shepard Books. This book is an honest account written by a 14-year-old of the overwhelming emotions after a boy witnesses his father being shot and fatally wounded. It includes accounts of the trial and its outcome. Ages 8 to 14.

Smith, I. (Ed.). (1991). *We Don't Like Remembering Them as a Field of Grass.* Portland, OR: The Dougy Center. A book by children of many ages telling of how they feel about a loved one being murdered. Ages 7 to 16.

## Books About AIDS

Balkwill, F. (1993). *Cell Wars.* London, England: William Collins & Sons. This story for young children uses words and pictures to thoroughly explain cells, viruses, and good and bad cells. Ages 5 to 9.

Fassler, D., & McQueen, K. (1990). *The Kids Book About AIDS.* Burlington, VT: Waterfront Books. This book approaches the subject of AIDS in a sensitive manner to which young children can relate. Kids can use it as a workbook. Ages 4 to 8.

Girard, L. (1991). *Alex, the Kid with AIDS.* Morton Grove, IL: Albert Whitman & Co. This is a story about a fourth-grade boy who has AIDS and the friendships he creates. Ages 6 to 11.

Hausherr, R. (1989). *Children and the AIDS Virus.* New York, NY: Clarion Books. An informative book for older and younger children that tells and shows through pictures the world of AIDS. Ages 5 and up.

Jordan, M. (1989). *Losing Uncle Tim.* Niles, IL: A. Whitman Niles. Daniel's Uncle Tim dies of AIDS, and Daniel struggles with many feelings about it.

McNaught, D. (1993). *The Gift of Good-Bye: A Workbook for Children Who Love Someone with AIDS.* New York, NY: Dell Publishing. This is an interactive book to help adults and children deal with the painful experience of loving someone with AIDS. Ages 5 to 10.

Merrifield, M. (1990). *Come Sit by Me.* Ontario, Canada: Women's Press. A great book for parents and teachers to educate young children on facts about AIDS. Ages 4 to 8.

Moutoussamy-Ashe, J. (1993). *Daddy and Me.* New York, NY: Alfred A. Knopf. A wonderful photo story of Arthur Ashe and his daughter Camera and their journey with AIDS. Ages 4 through adulthood.

Sanford, D. (1991). *David Has AIDS.* Portland, OR: Multnomah Press. David struggles with the disease of AIDS. Ages 7 to 11.

Wiener, L., & Pizzo, P. A. (1994). *Be a Friend.* Morton Grove, IL: Albert Whitman and Co. A wonderful book written by children with AIDS and presented by people whose daily work is helping these children. Ages 5 through adulthood.

## Books About Child Abuse

Loftis, C. (1995). *The Words Hurt.* Far Hills, NJ: New Horizon Press. A story for young children explaining how words can be hurtful and abusive and what children can do about it.

Naylor, P. R. (1991). *Shiloh.* New York, NY: Atheneum Children's Books. The story about Shiloh, an abused dog, and the boy who loved him. Ages 8 to 12.

Pall, M., & Streit, L. (1983). *Let's Talk About It: The Book for Children About Child Abuse.* Saratoga, CA: R & E Publishers. A simple book defining child abuse and using cartoon illustrations that question children on understandings. Ages 9 to 14.

## Book About Satanic Ritual Abuse

Sanford, D. (1990). *Don't Make Me Go Back, Mommy.* Portland, OR: Multnomah Press. A book explaining satanic rituals to children and ways for caring adults to work with kids who have experienced these rituals. Ages 6 to 10.

## Books About Foster Homes

Nasta, P. (1991). *Aaron Goes to the Shelter.* Tucson, AZ: Whole Child. A story and workbook about children who have experienced family chaos and may be placed in a shelter or foster care. Ages 6 to 12.

Sanford, D. (1993). *For Your Own Good.* Sisters, OR: Questar Publishers. A book for children about foster care and ways that caregivers can help. Ages 6 to 10.

## Book About Homelessness

Powell, S. (1992). *A Chance to Grow.* Minneapolis, MN: Carolrhoda Books. Joe, his mom, and his sister Gracey are evicted from their apartment. They are left homeless and live on the streets and in shelters seeking a permanent home. Ages 6 to 11.

## Books About Sexual Abuse

Girard, L. (1984). *My Body Is Private.* Morton Grove, IL: Albert Whitman and Co. A direct approach to help children distinguish between good touching and bad touching, including help for parents. Ages 5 to 10.

Russell, P., & Stone, B. (1986). *Do You Have a Secret?* Minneapolis, MN: CompCare Publishers. This book helps adults talk to children about sexual abuse and explains how they can seek help. Ages 4 to 8.

Sanford, D. (1986). *I Can't Talk About It.* Portland, OR: Multnomah Press. Annie talks to an abstract form, Love, about her sexual abuse and begins to heal and trust. Ages 8 to 13.

Sanford, D. (1993). *Something Must Be Wrong with Me*. Portland, OR: Multnomah Press. This is the story of Dino, a boy who is sexually abused. He finds the courage to talk about it. Ages 7 to 12.

## Books About Violence in the Home

Berstein, S. *A Family That Fights*. Morton Grove, IL: Albert Whitman & Co. A story about a family's domestic violence and ways children and adults can get help. Ages 5 to 9.

Cohen, J. (1994). *Why Did It Happen?* New York, NY: Morrow Junior Books. This is a story about a boy who witnesses a violent crime in his neighborhood. The author provides ways to cope. Ages 6 to 11.

Davis, D. (1984). *Something Is Wrong in My House*. Seattle, WA: Parenting Press. A book about parents fighting, ways to cope with violence, and how to break the cycle. Ages 8 to 12.

Hochban, T., & Krykorka, V. (1994). *Hear My Roar: A Story of Family Violence*. New York, NY: Annick Press Ltd. This book is the story of Lungin, a little boy bear whose dad is violently abusive. Lungin and his mom choose to take action and go to a shelter as a first step. Ages 7 to 12. Can be read to younger children.

Paris, S. (1986). *Mommy and Daddy Are Fighting*. Seattle, WA: Seals Press. Honest discussion of parental fighting, with a guide for parents. Ages 5 to 8.

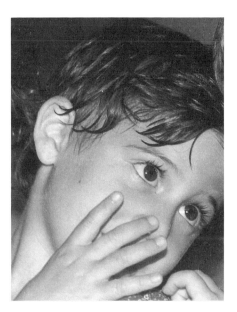

Sanford, D. (1989). *Lisa's Parents Fight*. Portland, OR: Multnomah Press. The story of 10-year-old Lisa, her siblings, and parents who interact with angry outbursts and occasional physical abuse. Ages 8 to 12.

Winston-Hiller, R. (1986). *Some Secrets Are for Sharing*. Denver, CO: MAC Publishing. A story of a family secret of a boy being beaten by his mom. He finally tells and gets help for himself and his mom. Ages 6 to 11.

## Book About Trauma

Berry, J. (1990). *About Traumatic Experiences*. Chicago, IL: Children's Press. Answers to kids' questions about trauma and traumatic experiences. Ages 8 to 11.

**Book About Weight Disorders and Eating Problems**

Berry, J. (1990). *About Weight Problems and Eating Disorders.* Chicago, IL: Children's Press. An interesting book that explains the realities of eating disorders and weight problems. Ages 7 to 13.

**Books About Stranger Anxiety**

Girard, L. (1985). *Who Is a Stranger and What Should I Do?* Morton Grove, IL: Albert Whitman & Co. This book explains in simple language what a stranger is and what kids can do in different situations. Ages 6 to 10.

Schaefer, C. (1992). *Cat's Got Your Tongue.* New York, NY: Magination Press. This is the story of Anna, a kindergartner diagnosed as an electively mute child. Children with stranger anxieties also can relate to Anna's behaviors. Ages 3 to 7.

**Books About Adult Illness**

Dorfman, E. (1994). *The C-Word.* Portland, OR: New Sage Press. This book presents family interviews and photographs about their cancer experience. For teenagers.

Goodman, M. B. (1991). *Vanishing Cookies.* Mississauga, Canada: Arthur Jones Lithographing Ltd. A book that talks honestly about a parent's cancer treatment. Ages 6 to 13.

Hazouri, S., & McLaughlin, M. (1994). *My Family Is Living with Cancer.* Warminster, PA: Mar*co Products. This is a helpful resource for children and families to understand and cope with a serious illness. Accompanying workbook available. Ages 3 to 10.

Heegaard, M. (1991). *When Someone Has a Very Special Illness.* Minneapolis, MN: Woodland Press. A practical and interactive workbook that addresses feelings when a loved one is very sick. Ages 6 to 12.

LeShan, E. (1986). *When a Parent Is Very Sick.* Boston, MA: Joy Street Books. A helpful book for children and parents that talks openly about the stress of having a parent with a serious illness. Ages 8 to 13.

Nystrom, C. (1990). *Emma Says Goodbye.* Batavia, IL: Lion Publisher. Emma's aunt has a terminal illness, and she comes to live with Emma. Ages 8 to 14.

Parkinson, C. (1991). *My Mommy Has Cancer.* Rochester, NY: Park Press. This book helps young children learn about cancer, its treatment, and its emotional impact. Ages 4 to 8.

Strauss, L. (1988). *Coping When a Parent Has Cancer.* New York: Rosen Publishing. A book for teenagers who are coping with a parent with cancer.

## Books About Children's Illness

Baznik, D. (1981). *Becky's Story.* Bethesda, MD: Association for the Care of Children's Health. Becky, a 6-year-old, feels confused and left out when her brother is in a bad accident and she feels he is given all the attention. Ages 4 to 7.

Gaes, J. (1989). *My Book for Kids with Cansur.* Pierre, SD: Melius-Peterson. The story of 8-year-old Jason who successfully battles cancer. Jason's brothers illustrate the book. Ages 7 to 12.

Lawrence, M. (1987). *My Life: Melinda's Story.* Alexandria, VA: Children's Hospice International. A story by Melinda about her journey through illness. Ages 5 and up.

Maple, M. (1992). *On the Wings of a Butterfly.* Seattle, WA: Parenting Press. A butterfly becomes a friend to Lisa, a child dying of cancer. Lisa shares her fears of dying. Ages 5 to 10.

Schultz, C. M. (1990). *Why, Charlie Brown, Why?* New York: Topper Books. The story about Charlie's friend Janice, who has leukemia, and what happens when a friend is very ill. Ages 5 to 10.

Sanford, D. (1992). *No Longer Afraid.* Sisters, OR: Multnomah Press. A story about Jaimie, a young girl with cancer, and her journey with this critical illness. Ages 7 to 11.

Stolp, H. (1990). *The Golden Bird.* New York: Dial Books. An 11-year-old boy is terminally ill and explores his thoughts and feelings about death.

## Books About War/Death

Bunting, E. (1990). *The Wall.* New York, NY: Clarion Books. Illustrations and story about a father and son who visit the Vietnam Veterans Memorial and the impact of three generations of war. Ages 5 to 8.

Coerr, E. (1977). *Sadako and the Thousand Paper Cranes.* New York, NY: Putnam. This is a true story about a Japanese girl who is dying from her exposure to radiation from the bomb at Hiroshima. Her hope for peace and life is symbolized in her paper cranes. Ages 8 to 13.

Finkelstein, N. (1985). *Remember Not to Forget.* New York, NY: Mulberry Books. This book describes clearly for young children the history and origins of the holocaust in Nazi Germany. Ages 6 to 10.

## Books About Drugs

Sanford, D. (1987). *I Can Say No.* Portland, OR: Multnomah Press. David's story about his feelings concerning his older brother's involvement with drugs. Ages 6 to 10.

Taylor, C. (1992). *The House That Crack Built.* San Francisco, CA: Chronicle Books. A poetic story for young children that explores today's drug problems. Ages 7 to 12.

## Books About Families with Alcoholics

Black, C. (1982). *My Dad Loves Me, My Dad Has a Disease.* Denver, CO: MAC Publishing. This is a workbook for children of alcoholics to help them better understand alcoholism and their feelings about it. Ages 6 to 14.

Carbone, E. L. (1992). *My Dad's Definitely Not a Drunk.* Burlington, VT: Waterfront Books. Corey is a 12-year-old boy who struggles with the secret that his dad drinks too much. Corey and his mom discover a way to get help. Ages 9 to 14.

Hastings, J., & Typpo, M. (1984). *An Elephant in the Living Room.* Minneapolis, MN: CompCare Publishers. A workbook about alcoholism that allows children to express their feelings. Ages 8 to 12.

Sanford, D. (1984). *I Know the World's Worst Secret.* Portland, OR: Multnomah Press. A girl talks about her alcoholic mom. Ages 8 to 13.

Vigna, J. (1988). *I Wish Daddy Didn't Drink So Much.* Morton Grove, IL: Albert Whitman & Co. The story of a little girl who constantly is disappointed by her dad's drinking. With help from caring adults, she gains new hope in her situation. Ages 4 to 8.

## Books About Dad's Leaving

Cochran, V. (1992). *My Daddy Is a Stranger.* Omaha, NE: Centering Corporation. The story of a little girl whose dad left home when she was a baby and how she feels and explains his absence. Ages 5 to 8.

Hickman, M. (1990). *When Andy's Father Went to Prison.* Niles, IL: Albert Whitman and Co. Andy's dad was arrested for stealing and put into prison. Andy copes with his feelings of shame and abandonment while his dad is away. Ages 5 to 9.

Lindsay, J. (1993). *Do I Have a Daddy?* Buena Park, CA: Morning Glory Press. The story of a single-parent child whose parents had never married and father is totally absent. It contains a special section for single parents. Ages 5 to 8.

## Books About Moving

Blume, J. (1986). *Are You There,God? It's Me, Margaret.* New York, NY: Dell Publishing. Margaret has to face moving and a new life. Ages 9 to 12.

McKend, H. (1988). *Moving Gives Me a Stomach Ache.* Ontario, Canada: Black Moss Press. The story of a child's anxiety and fear of moving. Ages 5 to 8.

## Books About Divorce

Boulden, J., & Boulden, J. (1991). *Let's Talk.* Santa Rosa, CA: Boulden Publishing. A kids' activity book for separation and divorce. Ages 5 to 8.

Evans, M. D. (1989). *This Is Me and My Single Parent.* New York, NY: Magination Press. A discovery workbook for children and single parents. Ages 8 to 13.

Fassler, D., Lash, M., & Ives, S. (1988). *Changing Families.* Burlington, VT: Waterfront Books. Advice for kids coping with divorce and remarriage. Ages 4 to 12.

Heegaard, M. (1990). *When Mom and Dad Separate.* Minneapolis, MN: Woodland Press. A workbook for children exploring thoughts and feelings about separation and divorce. Ages 6 to 12.

Krementz, J. (1988). *How It Feels When Parents Divorce.* New York, NY: Knopf. Many children describe how divorce has affected them. Ages 8 to 13.

Sanford, D. (1985). *Please Come Home.* Portland, OR: Multnomah Press. Jenny's thoughts and feelings are expressed to her teddy bear about her parents' divorce. Ages 7 to 12.

## Books About Adoption

Banish, R., & Jordan-Wong, J. (1992). *A Forever Family.* New York, NY: HarperCollins. Eight-year-old Jennifer was in many foster homes before being adopted as a part of her forever family. Ages 5 to 8.

Girard, L. (1989). *We Adopted You Benjamin Koo.* Morton Grove, IL: Albert Whitman & Co. Benjamin is a 9-year-old boy from another country. He tells of how he adjusted to adoption and a culturally blended family. Ages 5 to 10.

Sanford, D. (1989). *Brian Was Adopted.* Portland, OR: Multnomah Press. Brian questions many parts of adoption and talks to God about it. Ages 7 to 11.

Stinson, K. (1992). *Steven's Baseball Mitt.* Ontario, Canada: Annick Press Ltd. Describes the thoughts and feelings that go through an adopted child's mind about his birth mother. Ages 5 to 8.

## Book About Natural Disaster

Williams, V. (1992). *A Chair for My Mother.* New York, NY: Mulberry Books. After a fire destroys their home, Rosa, her mom, and grandmother save their money for a big chair to share. Ages 5 to 10.

## Books About Feelings

Blackburn, L. (1991). *I Know I Made It Happen.* Omaha, NE: Centering Corporation. This book presents different circumstances where children find themselves feeling guilty and responsible for making things happen. Ages 5 to 8.

Crary, E. (1992). *I'm Mad.* Seattle, WA: Parenting Press. A children's book that identifies feelings and gives options on what to do with them. Ages 3 to 8.

Doleski, T. (1983). *The Hurt.* Mahwah, NJ: Paulist Press. The wonderful story about a little boy who keeps all of his hurts inside, until the hurt grows so big it fills his room. When he shares his feelings, the hurt begins to go away. All ages.

Hazen, B. (1992). *Even If I Did Something Awful.* New York, NY: Aladdin Books. The reassuring story of a little girl who realizes mom will love her no matter what she does. Ages 5 to 8.

Jampolsky, G., & Cirincione, D. (1991). *"Me First" and the Gimme Gimmes.* Deerfield Beach, FL: Health Communications. A story that shows the transformation of selfishness into love. All ages.

Kaufman, G., & Raphael, L. (1990). *Stick up for Yourself.* Minneapolis, MN: Free Spirit Publishing. A guide to help kids feel personal power and self-esteem. Ages 8 to 12.

Moser, A. (1988). *Don't Pop Your Cork on Monday.* Kansas City, MO: Landmark Editions. A handbook for children to explore the causes of stress and techniques to deal with it. Ages 5 to 8.

Moser, A. (1991). *Don't Feed the Monster on Tuesday.* Kansas City, MO: Landmark Editions. Dr. Moser offers children information on the importance of knowing their own self-worth and ways to improve self-esteem. Ages 5 to 8.

Munsch, R., & Martchenko, M. (1985). *Thomas' Snowsuit.* Ontario, Canada: Annick Press Ltd. A story about a child who refuses to wear his snowsuit and will not be manipulated by adults. Ages 5 to 8.

Oram, H. (1982). *Angry Arthur.* New York, NY: E.P. Dutton. Arthur becomes enraged with his mom and creates havoc on the planet. Ages 5 to 8.

Sanford, D. (1986). *Don't Look at Me.* Portland, OR: Multnomah Press. The story of Patrick, who feels very stupid and learns to feel special about himself. Ages 7 to 11.

Seuss, Dr. (1990). *Oh, the Places You'll Go.* New York, NY: Random House. Dr. Seuss uses his magical creativity to inspire young and old to succeed in life, despite the many ups and downs they face. Ages 5 through adulthood.

Simon, N. (1989). *I Am Not a Crybaby.* New York, NY: Puffin Books. This book shows how children of different races and cultures share the commonality of feelings. Ages 5 to 8.

Steig, W. (1988). *Spinky Sulks.* New York: Sunburst Books. Spinky is angry and begins to sulk. No one can make him stop until he is ready. Ages 5 to 8.

Voirst, J. (1972). *Alexander and the Terrible Horrible No Good Very Bad Day.* New York, NY: Aladdin Books. Alexander has a day where everything goes wrong. Everyone can relate to this. Ages 5 to 8.

Voirst, J. (1981). *If I Were in Charge of the World and Other Worries.* New York, NY: Aladdin Books. A book of poems for children expressing how kids feel about a lot of things. Ages 5 and up.

## Books About Nightmares

Devlin, W., & Devlin, H. (1994). *Maggie Has a Nightmare.* New York, NY: Macmillan. Maggie's daytime fears appear in her dreams. Sharing them helps her fears disappear. Ages 4 to 7.

Lobby, T. (1990). *Jessica and the Wolf.* New York, NY: Magination Press. Jessica's parents help her solve the problem of her recurring nightmare. Ages 4 to 8.

McGuire, L. (1994). *Nightmares in the Mist.* Palo Alto, CA: Enchanté Publishing. Alicia has many fears since her mom went into the hospital. Magical paint helps her overcome them. Ages 5 to 9.

Marcus, I., & Marcus, P. (1990). *Scary Night Visitors.* New York, NY: Magination Press. Davey has fears at night and learns to feel safe through experiencing his feelings directly. Ages 4 to 7.

## Books About Funerals and Memorial Services

Ancona, G. (1993). *Pablo Remembers.* New York, NY: Lothrop, Lee & Shepard Books. A beautiful book with wonderful photographs that explains the Mexican fiesta of The Day of the Dead, which celebrates the life of lost loved ones each year. Ages 6 to 11.

Balter, L. (1991). *A Funeral for Whiskers.* Hauppauge, NY: Barron's Educational Series. Sandy's cat dies, and she finds useful ways to express her feelings and commemorate. Ages 5 to 9.

Carson, J. (1992). *You Hold Me and I'll Hold You.* New York, NY: Orchard Books. A soft story for young children about a little girl's feelings of wanting to hold and be held at a memorial service. Ages 5 to 9.

Johnson, J., & Johnson, M. (1990). *Tell Me, Papa.* Omaha, NE: Centering Corporation. This book simply and clearly explains how kids feel about death, burial, and funerals. Ages 6 to 10.

Jukes, M. (1993). *I'll See You in My Dreams.* New York, NY: Alfred A. Knopf. A little girl prepares to visit a seriously ill uncle and imagines writing a farewell message across the sky. Ages 5 to 10.

Kloeppel, D. (1981). *Sam's Grandma.* College Park, PA: Author. A 7-year-old boy tells his story of his Grandma's death and subsequent funeral. Kids can color in it. Ages 4 to 8.

Techner, D., & Hirt-Manheimer, J. (1993). *A Candle for Grandpa: A Guide to the Jewish Funeral for Children and Parents.* New York: UAHC Press. A book simply written for children to explain Jewish funeral and burial practices. Ages 7 to 12.

Death and transformation are man's unchosen and unchangeable fate. All that he can choose and change is consciousness. But to change this is to change all.

*Rodney Collin*
Campbell, 1991

# REFERENCES

Adler, J. (1994, January 10). Kids growing up scared. *Newsweek,* 43–50.

Ancona, G. (1993). *Pablo remembers.* New York: Lothrop, Lee & Shepard Books.

Bernstein, S. (1991). *A family that fights.* Morton Grove, IL: Albert Whitman & Company.

Blackburn, L. (1991). *I know I made it happen: A book about children and guilt.* Omaha, NE: Centering Corporation.

Bode, J. (1993). *Death is hard to live with.* New York: Bantam Doubleday Dell.

Braza, K. (1988). *Memory book for bereaved children.* Salt Lake City, UT: Healing Resources.

Campbell, E. (Ed.). (1991). *A dancing star: Inspirations to guide and heal.* San Francisco, CA: Aquarian Press.

Carson, J. (1992). *You hold me and I'll hold you.* New York: Orchard Books.

Cassini, K., & Rogers, J. (1990). *Death and the classroom.* Cincinnati, OH: Griefwork of Cincinnati.

Centers for Disease Control and Prevention. (1995, June). *HIV/AIDS Surveillance Report, 7*(1), 12–14.

Cohen, J. (1994). *Why did it happen?* New York: Morrow Junior Books.

Crary, E. (1992). *I'm mad.* Seattle, WA: Parenting Press.

Cunningham, L. (1990). *Teen age grief (TAG).* Panorama, CA: Teen Age Grief.

Davis, N. (1990). *Once upon a time: Therapeutic stories.* Oxon Hill, MD: Psychological Associates of Oxon Hill.

Doleski, T. (1983). *The hurt.* Mahwah, NJ: Paulist Press.

Dorfman, E. (1994). *The C-word.* Portland, OR: New Sage Press.

Fanos, J., & Wiener, L. (1994, June). Tomorrow's survivors: Siblings of Human Immunodeficiency Virus infected children. *Developmental and Behavioral Pediatrics, 15*(3), 43.

Fassler, D. (1990). *What's a virus anyway?* Burlington, VT: Waterfront Books.

Fox, S. (1988). *Good grief: Helping groups of children when a friend dies.* Boston: New England Association for the Education of Young Children.

Gil, E. (1991). *The healing power of play.* New York: The Guilford Press.

Gliko-Bradon, M. (1992). *Grief comes to class.* Omaha, NE: Centering Corporation.

Goldman, L. (1994). *Life and loss: A guide to help grieving children.* Muncie, IN: Accelerated Development.

Gootman, M. (1994). *When a friend dies.* Minneapolis, MN: Free Spirit Publishing.

Heegaard, M. (1988). *When someone very special dies.* Minneapolis, MN: Woodland Press.

Henderson, R. (1995, January/February). Caught in the crossfire. *Common Boundary,* 28–35.

Henry-Jenkins, W. (1993). *Just us.* Omaha, NE: Centering Corporation.

Hochban, T., & Krykorka, V. (1994). *Hear my roar: A story of family violence.* New York: Annick Press.

Hughes, L. (1994). *Collected poems.* New York: Alfred A. Knopf.

Johnson, J., & Johnson, M. (1990). *Tell me, Papa*. Omaha, NE: Centering Corporation.

Klicker, R. (1990). *A student dies, a school mourns . . . Are you prepared?* Buffalo, NY: Thanos Institute.

Leenaars, A., & Wenckstern, S. (1991). *Suicide prevention in schools*. New York: Hemisphere.

Lobby, T. (1990). *Jessica and the wolf*. New York: Magination Press.

Loftis, C. (1995). *The words hurt*. Far Hills, NJ: New Horizon Press.

MacLean, G. (1990). *Suicide in children and adolescents*. Lewiston, NY: Hogrefe & Huber Publishers.

Mahon, K. L. (1992). *Just one tear*. New York: Lothrop, Lee, and Shepard Books.

Merrifield, M. (1990). *Come sit by me*. Ontario, Canada: Women's Press.

*Morbidity and Mortality Weekly Report*. (1994, August 26). (p. 43).

Moser, A. (1988). *Don't pop your cork on Monday*. Kansas City, MO: Landmark Editions.

Moutassamy-Ashe, J. (1993). *Daddy and me*. New York: Alfred A. Knopf.

National Committee for the Prevention of Child Abuse. (1994, January 10). In J. Adler, Kids growing up scared. *Newsweek*, 43–50.

Naylor, P. R. (1991). *Shiloh*. New York: Atheneum Children's Books.

Oates, M. (1993). *Death in the school community*. Alexandria, VA: American Counseling Association.

O'Toole, D. (1988). *Aarvy Aardvark finds hope*. Burnsville, NC: Mt. Rainbow Publications.

O'Toole, D. (1989). *Growing through grief: A K-12 curriculum to help young people through all kinds of grief.* Burnsville, NC: Mt. Rainbow Publications.

O'Toole, D. (1994). *Aarvy Aardvark finds hope* (video). Burnsville, NC: Mt. Rainbow Publications.

Pall, M., & Streit, L. B. (1983). *Let's talk about it: The book for children about child abuse.* Saratoga, CA: R & E Publishers.

Roberts, J., & Johnson, J. (1994). *Thank you for coming to say good-bye.* Omaha, NE: Centering Corporation.

Russell, P., & Stone, B. (1986). *Do you have a secret?* Minneapolis, MN: CompCare Publishers.

Ryan, M. (1994, October 9). What our children need is adults who care. *Parade Magazine.*

Sanford, D. (1986). *I can't talk about it.* Portland, OR: Multnomah Press.

Schaefer, C. (1992). *Cat's got your tongue.* New York: Magination Press.

Smith, I. (Ed.). (1991). *We don't like remembering them as a field of grass.* Portland, OR: The Dougy Center.

Smith, J. (1989). *Suicide prevention.* Holmes Beach, FL: Learning Publications.

Stein, S. (1974). *About dying.* New York: Walker and Company.

Techner, D., & Hirt-Manheimer, J. (1993). *A candle for Grandpa: A guide to the Jewish funeral for children and parents.* New York: UAHC Press.

Tongue, B. J. (1982). *The international book of family therapy.* New York: Brunner/Mazel.

Traisman, E. (1992). *Fire in my heart, ice in my veins.* Omaha, NE: Centering Corporation.

Traisman, E. (1994). *A child remembers.* Omaha, NE: Centering Corporation.

U.S. Advisory Board on Child Abuse and Neglect. (1995, April). *Nation's shame: Fatal child abuse and neglect in U.S.* Washington, DC: Author.

U.S. Department of Health and Human Services. (1994, November 14). In D. Van Biema, Parents who kill. *Time,* p. 50.

Van Biema, D. (1994, November 14). Parents who kill. *Time,* 50–51.

Ward, B. (1993). *Good grief.* London: Jessica Kingsley.

Webb, N. B. (1993). *Helping bereaved children.* New York: The Guilford Press.

Wiener, L. S., Best, A., & Pizzo, P. A. (1994). *Be a friend: Children who live with HIV speak.* Morton Grove, IL: Albert Whitman & Company.

Wiener, L., Fair, C., & Pizzo, P. A. (1993). Care for the child with HIV infection and AIDS. In A. Armstrong-Dailey & S. Z. Goltzer (Eds.), *Hospice care for children* (pp. 85–104). New York: Oxford Press.

*Yankelovich Youth Monitor.* (1994, January 10). In J. Adler, Kids growing up scared. *Newsweek*, p. 50.

# INDEX

# ABOUT THE AUTHOR

Linda Goldman is the author of *Life and Loss: A Guide to Help Grieving Children.* She has been an educator in the public school system for almost 20 years, in both teaching and counseling capacities.

Presently Linda is a certified grief therapist and certified grief educator who practices near Washington, DC. A creative therapist, Linda began her private grief practice after the death of her stillborn daughter, Jennifer. Working with grieving children, teenagers, and adults, Linda finds gentle and innovative ways to work through the pain and confusion of loss and grief. She has developed special expertise in the area of prenatal loss, as well as an ability to identify and normalize complicated grief issues.

The success of her grief work has led her to educate other caring adults through workshops in school systems and universities on ways to help children with normal and complicated grief. Linda lives in Chevy Chase, MD, with her husband, Michael, and son, Jonathan.